America First?
Isolationism in U.S. Foreign Policy From the 19th to the 21st Century

Stefan Klein

America First?

Isolationism in U.S. Foreign Policy From the 19th to the 21st Century

Stefan Klein

2017

Carola Hartmann Miles-Verlag

CIP-Kurztitelaufnahme der Deutschen Nationalbibliothek:
Stefan Klein, America First? Isolationism in U.S. Foreign Policy From the 19th to the 21st Century, Berlin 2017

ISBN 978-3-945861-66-0

© Carola Hartmann Miles-Verlag,
(www.miles-verlag.jimdo.com;
email: miles-verlag@t-online.de)

Herstellung: Books on Demand GmbH, Norderstedt

Titelbild: Jeff Swensen/Getty Images News/Getty Images
Alle Rechte, insbesondere das Recht der Vervielfältigung und Verbreitung sowie der Übersetzung, vorbehalten. Kein Teil des Werkes darf in irgendeiner Form (durch Fotokopie, Mikrofilm oder ein anderes Verfahren) ohne schriftliche Genehmigung des Verlages reproduziert oder unter Verwendung elektronischer Systeme gespeichert, verarbeitet, vervielfältigt oder verbreitet werden.

Printed in Germany

ABSTRACT

During the 2016 election campaign, President Donald J. Trump championed a policy of intervention and isolation in U.S. foreign policy, which aroused fears among European North Atlantic Treaty Organization (NATO) allies about U.S. commitments to collective defense. This contentious issue points to a preference in certain political circles for an end to U.S. interventionism, which, from a foreign policy perspective, seems tantamount to isolationism.

This book examines isolationism in the experience of statecraft and considers the potential implications of this nation's deeply rooted isolationist tendencies for continued U.S. security commitments to NATO. To trace the evolution of isolationism, this work analyzes case studies of U.S. decision-making prior to entering the First and Second World Wars, U.S. involvement in NATO after the Second World War, and resistance within the Senate to large numbers of U.S. troops in Europe in the 1960s and 1970s. The analysis includes consideration of congressional partisanship, public opinion, and domestic political issues in the shaping of U.S. foreign policy.

This volume concludes that domestic political issues dominate the conduct of U.S. foreign policy. The political agenda of the 2016 Trump campaign, as well as the first days of the administration, mirrored debates of the past, which should not surprise experts of U.S. political history.

TABLE OF CONTENTS

I.		**INTRODUCTION**	13
	A.	**Framing the Problem—2016 U.S. Election Campaign**	13
	B.	**Research Question and Focus of this Work**	15
	C.	**Literature Review**	16
	D.	**Research Design and Overview**	19
II.		**THE CHALLENGES OF THE TWO WORLD WARS**	21
	A.	**The Path to the First World War and its Aftermath**	21
		1. Historical Overview	21
		2. November 1912 to June 1914—Preludes to War	23
		3. June 1914 to April 1917—American Neutrality and Entering the War	26
		4. April 1917 to October 1918—Wilson's Ideas for a New Internationalism	35
		5. October 1918 to March 1920—Messy Peace and the Defeat of Wilsonianism	37
	B.	**The Interwar Period and the Prelude to the Second World War**	42
		1. Historical Overview	43
		2. April 1921 to February 1932—Economic Prosperity and False Security	44
		3. February 1932 to May 1937—The Height of Isolationism	47
		4. July 1937 to June 1940—The End of Neutrality	56

		5. June 1940 to December 1941—America's Entry into the War	64
III.		**DEALING WITH A NEW RESPONSIBILITY — U.S. FOREIGN POLICY AFTER THE SECOND WORLD WAR**	**75**
	A.	**The Path to NATO—U.S. Responsibility for European Security**	75
		1. Historical Overview	76
		2. September 1945 to December 1947—U.S. Domestic Political Situation and the Emergence of the Cold War	77
		3. December 1947 to March 1948—The Brussels Pact	82
		4. March 1948 to April 1949—The Path to NATO	86
		5. April 1949 to June 1950—Implementing the Treaty and the Military Aid Program	89
		6. June 1950 to April 1951—The Great Debate	93
	B.	**The Mansfield Resolutions—Opposition to High Levels of U.S. Troops in Europe**	101
		1. Historical Overview	101
		2. August 1966 to September 1970—Mansfield's Resolutions	108
		3. May 1971 to November 1971—Mansfield's Strategy Change	114
		4. April 1973 to September 1973—Peak of Pressure	117
		5. June 1974 to June 1975—Final Defeat	119

IV.		CONCLUSION	123
	A.	**Testing the Hypotheses**	123
		1. Variations of Isolationism in the Historic Context	124
		2. Influence of Domestic Policy	127
		3. U.S. Leadership Role	131
	B.	**Implications for Current U.S. Security Commitments to Europe and NATO**	132
		1. Rhetoric of the 2016 Election Campaign and the New Trump Administration	132
		2. Continuities and Discontinuities	135
		3. Final Remarks	138

		APPENDIX	141
	A.	**Washington's Farewell Address**	141
	B.	**The Monroe Doctrine**	143
	C.	**George F. Kennan's Containment Policy**	143

		LIST OF REFERENCES	145

LIST OF ACRONYMS AND ABBREVIATIONS

CDA	Committee to Defend America by Aiding the Allies
FDR	Franklin Delano Roosevelt
FED	Federal Reserve
HR	House Resolution
NAC	North Atlantic Council
NATO	North Atlantic Treaty Organization
NSC	National Security Council
MBFR	Mutual and Balanced Force Reductions
SACEUR	Supreme Allied Commander Europe
SALT	Strategic Arms Limitation Talks
SHAPE	Supreme Headquarters Atlantic Powers in Europe
UN	United Nations
USS	United States Ship
WILPF	Women's International League for Peace and Freedom

ACKNOWLEDGEMENTS

I express my sincere gratitude to Dr. Donald Abenheim and Dr. Carolyn Halladay for sharing their expertise on U.S. foreign policy. Both encouraged my interest in the U.S. history, which is the key to understanding the country's policy toward Europe and NATO. Their mentorship, rigorous evaluation, and honest appraisal helped shape the final product for the better.

Additionally, I would like to thank my wife, Claudia, and my daughters, Johanna and Elisabeth, for their support and patience during my extended working hours as a student at Naval Postgraduate School.

I. INTRODUCTION

A. Framing the Problem—2016 U.S. Election Campaign

Despite the 2014 U.S. pivot to Europe in the wake of the Crimean annexation, the tumultuous 2016 U.S. presidential election campaign aroused fears among European North Atlantic Treaty Organization (NATO) members about U.S. commitments to collective defense. One of President Donald J. Trump's central contentions was that the European allies should take a greater share of the security burden; otherwise, they must defend themselves.[1] Other prominent figures piled on, calling into question the most basic logic of the alliance. For example, in reference to the Baltics, former Speaker of the U.S. House of Representatives Newt Gingrich announced that he would not risk a nuclear war over some place in "the suburbs of St. Petersburg."[2]

Trump's campaign rhetoric was likely designed to raise questions about the U.S. commitment to NATO. Nonetheless, Trump's words revived the debate over interventionism versus isolationism in U.S. foreign policy, and led his opponent Hillary Clinton to describe him as a "dangerous isolationist," according to *Washington Post* correspondent Anne Gearan.[3] But, is *isolationism* the right term? Political scientist David Hastings Dunn explains that the mainstream political discourse in foreign policy focuses on the role of the United States in the international system of states.[4] He further writes that the terms isolationism

---

[1] Donald J. Trump, "Trump on Foreign Policy," *National Interest*, April 27, 2016, http://nationalinterest.org/feature/trump-foreign-policy-15960.

[2] Reena Flores, "Newt Gingrich: NATO Countries 'Ought to Worry' about U.S. Commitment," *CBS News*, July 21, 2016, http://www.cbsnews.com/news/newt-gingrich-trump-would-reconsider-his-obligation-to-nato/.

[3] Anne Gearan, "Clinton Slams Trump as a Dangerous Isolationist in American Legion Speech," *Washington Post*, August 31, 2016, https://www.washingtonpost.com/news/post-politics/wp/2016/08/31/clinton-plans to slam trump-as-a-dangerous-isolationist-in-american-legion-speech/.

[4] David Hastings Dunn, "Isolationism Revisited: Seven Persistent Myths in the Contemporary American Foreign Policy Debate," *Review of International Studies* 31, no. 2 (2005): 241, doi:10.1017IS0260210505006431.

and interventionism are loosely used to describe different, even opposing, approaches and isolationism is nothing more than "a straw man, an argument presented to be knocked down, and a bogeyman to spread fear that the ramparts of internationalism are about to be breached."[5] As a result, as Dunn asserts, the legacy of isolationism influences contemporary discussions and has been a recurrent theme.[6]

According to John Dumbrell, isolationist attitudes question U.S. core commitments to European security and alliances.[7] Furthermore, the "partisan political debate rarely achieves the sophistication of academic analysis."[8] Dunn asserts that contemporary debates misunderstand the historical context of U.S. isolationism, which evolved from the situation of the 17th and 18th centuries in which the young United States sought to isolate itself from the European great powers in North America to consolidate and pursue manifest destiny of continental expansion.[9] So, one can assert that today's misuse of the terminology in the political debate almost always illustrates a lack of knowledge about isolationism in U.S. statecraft. Trump's policy of reluctant interventionism in U.S. security affairs—at least in Europe—brought to the forefront a traditionally Republican and, indeed, American attitude of exceptionalism and isolation about foreign relations since the nation's founding.

As foreign politics has become more complex, the American electorate tends not to follow foreign policy in its particulars. In an article by journalists Max Fisher and Amanda Taub, political scientist Elizabeth N. Saunders explains that voters search for policy agendas based

---

[5] Dunn, "Isolationism Revisited," 243.

[6] Ibid., 237.

[7] John Dumbrell, "Varieties of Post-Cold War American Isolationism," *Government and Opposition* 34 (1999): 25, doi:10.1111/j.1477-7053.1999.tb00469.x.

[8] John Dumbrell, "American Isolationism: A Response to David Hastings Dunn," *Review of International Studies* 31, no. 4 (2005): 699, doi:10.1017/S0260210505006704.

[9] Dunn, "Isolationism Revisited," 260, 261.

on simple values, for instance, strength and inclusiveness, which provide easy solutions.[10] NATO requires cooperation. Thus, voters recognize Trump's warnings toward the alliance as an expression of strength, and the electorate seems unlikely to be interested in renegotiating the U.S. role in the alliance. In the same article, political scientist Colin Dueck asserts that voters are "feeling displaced by long-term trends toward cultural and economic globalization," and the "fear of change and desire for order at home" dominates the discussion.[11] Hence, Fisher and Taub argue that "Mr. Trump's foreign policy is not a foreign policy at all, but rather a vessel for reaching voters on a purely ideological level."[12]

Stephen Sestanovich asks the question: "Are U.S. voters becoming isolationist—or just more partisan?" and concludes that the U.S. public is not isolationist in the traditional sense. The electorate still favors an active U.S. role in world; however, there is strong disagreement about the way this role should be exercised, especially when it comes to such topics as globalization and military intervention.[13] To the extent that these two issues exemplified American power in the 20th century and continue to the present, this disagreement implies a preference in certain circles for an end to U.S. interventionism—which, from a foreign policy perspective—seems tantamount to isolationism or at least a greater U.S. distance from its allies, notably in NATO.

B. Research Question and Focus of this Work

Isolationism certainly pervades debates about U.S. foreign policy. In practice, domestic political issues strongly influence the role of the

---

[10] See Max Fisher and Amanda Taub, "How Donald Trump Hacked the Politics of Foreign Policy," *New York Times*, October 19, 2016, http://www.nytimes.com/2016/10/20/world/americas/donald-trump-foreign-policy.html?ref=world&_r=0.

[11] Ibid.

[12] Ibid.

[13] Stephen Sestanovich, "Are U.S. Voters Becoming Isolationist–or Just More Partisan?" *Wall Street Journal* (blog), October 11, 2016, http://blogs.wsj.com/washwire/2016/10/11/are-u-s-voters-becoming-isolationist-or-just-more-partisan/.

United States in security commitments to Europe. To this end, this volume focuses on case studies of the U.S. entanglement in the First and Second World Wars, as well as the U.S. involvement in NATO and the Great Debate of 1951, and the Mansfield Resolutions, which provide an insight into historical domestic and international political discussions. Ultimately, this work answers the question: What are the origins of isolationism in U.S. statecraft, and what implications does isolationism have for the ongoing U.S. security commitments to Europe and NATO?

C. Literature Review

The term isolationism has its roots in the age of total war in the 20th century and describes the pattern of U.S. foreign policy that avoided political or military interference, especially in Europe. According to historian George C. Herring, isolationism in U.S. statecraft became part of political terminology in the 20th century and was not a product of the early political debate of the 18th and 19th century.[14] Historian Manfred Jonas aligns with Herring and affirms that isolationism is a product of the scholarly debates of the early 1920s, the mid-1930s, the late 1940s, and the two decades thereafter about U.S. commitments, particularly in Europe.[15] He acknowledges that isolationism first became a definable political position when the early consensus of U.S. neutrality broke down from 1914 to 1916, which corresponded with the period of the First World War.[16] Thus, isolationism best describes "American policy between the two world wars, especially after 1934, when the U.S. Congress attempted to insulate the country from an increasingly dangerous world situation," Jonas asserts.[17] A major shift in U.S. foreign policy occurred at the end of the Second World War, when

---

[14] George C. Herring, *From Colony to Superpower: U.S. Foreign Relations Since 1776* (New York: Oxford University Press, 2008), 83.

[15] Manfred Jonas, "Isolationism," in *Encyclopedia of American Foreign Affairs*, 2nd ed., ed. Alexander DeConde, Richard Dean Burns, and Frederik Logevall (New York: Scribner, 2002), 337–38.

[16] Ibid., 341.

[17] Ibid., 337.

isolationism reappeared in the Great Debate of 1950–1951 over U.S. military commitments to Europe in the Cold War. The discussion finally centered not on the general necessity of the assistance but on the extent of the aid; neutrality was no longer an option for the United States, as Jonas writes.[18] He further points out that debates thereafter, which include America's containment policy toward the Soviets as well as the debates of the late 1960s and early 1970s about U.S. international commitments, were not isolationist per se since they did not question U.S. engagement but concentrated on defining foreign policy goals.[19] In other words, isolationism is a recurrent theme in the debates about the U.S. role in Europe.

Since the 1890s, and more so in the 20th century, these debates about international engagement were limited to the question of military intervention, and the question of whether to use force or diplomacy as a means of foreign policy caused acute dilemmas for the United States. Historian Gordon A. Craig and political scientist Alexander L. George explain that it "is part of conventional wisdom of statecraft" that force and diplomacy must complement each other since attempts to use only one of these approaches has proven to be ineffective.[20] Thus, it is important to understand the arguments and implications of these debates related to military commitments, especially in Europe.

Since foreign policy is closely intertwined with U.S. domestic policy, political decision-making does not operate as smoothly as one would expect. For instance, George F. Kennan asserts that "there is a close connection between foreign policy and internal policy."[21] Kennan has a damning verdict about U.S. foreign affairs:

> On the question of the machinery of government, we have seen that a good deal of our trouble seems to have stemmed from the extent to which the executive has

---

[18] Jonas, "Isolationism," 347–48.

[19] Ibid., 338.

[20] Gordon A. Craig and Alexander L. George, *Force and Statecraft: Diplomatic Problems of Our Time*, 3rd ed. (New York: Oxford University Press, 1995), 258.

[21] Quoted in John Lewis Gaddis, *Strategies of Containment: A Critical Appraisal of Postwar American Security Policy* (New York: Oxford University Press, 1982), 32.

felt itself beholden to short-term trends of public opinion in the country and from what we might call the erratic and subjective nature of public reaction to foreign-policy questions. ... I think the record indicates that in the short term our public opinion, or what passes for our public opinion in the thinking of official Washington, can be easily led astray into areas of emotionalism and subjectivity which make it a poor and inadequate guide for national action. ... We are probably condemned to ... "diplomacy by dilettantism."[22]

In other words, public opinion has a significant influence on the conduct of U.S. statecraft.

Consequently, public opinion moved into the focus of historians. For instance, in his critical analysis of President Woodrow Wilson's postwar foreign policy, Thomas A. Bailey pays special attention to the influence of public opinion and how it turned "an unexampled opportunity to make a lasting peace" into a failure.[23] Jean-Baptiste Duroselle, in his analysis of U.S. foreign policy in the period between 1913 and 1945, asserts that the American people saw power politics as something immoral; whereas European nations "sought to have a *Weltpolitik*," a majority of the U.S. public, opposed the active participation of its military in international affairs.[24] Therefore, the analysis in this work considers the influence of public opinion on the conduct of U.S. foreign policy.

Jussi M. Hanhimäki has analyzed U.S. statecraft during the Cold War and explains that domestic policy plays a central role in foreign affairs. He quotes historian Melvin Small who asserts that "the central role of domestic politics in determining American foreign policy has changed little since [President George] Washington's day, and if anything, has

---

[22] George F. Kennan, *American Diplomacy 1900–1950* (Chicago: University of Chicago Press, 1951), 81.

[23] Thomas A. Bailey, *Woodrow Wilson & The Lost Peace* (Chicago: Quadrangle, 1944), vi.

[24] Jean-Baptiste Duroselle, *From Wilson to Roosevelt: Foreign Policy of the United States 1913–1945* (Cambridge: Harvard University Press, 1963), vii.

increased in potency and complexity."[25] Hanhimäki identified certain fields of domestic policy that encouraged a "unilateral" tendency in American foreign policy: economy, ethnicity, election cycles, party politics, and morality.[26] Thus, the case study approach in this volume promises to direct a special focus on domestic policy and its effects on isolationist tendencies in U.S. foreign policy.

D. Research Design and Overview

This work follows three main hypotheses. First, debates about isolationism are not a new phenomenon. Instead, they are an essential element of U.S. foreign policy rooted in the country's historical traditions. Second, foreign policy is shaped, to a high degree, by domestic political issues. Third, America has an imposed leadership role in the Western hemisphere as a promoter of security and democratic values—especially toward Europe—due to its economic and military predominance. With these hypotheses in mind, the research objective of this work follows an idiographic approach that highlights the unique elements of the isolationist view in U.S. foreign policy debate.

As the debate about U.S. engagement culminates in the question of the use of military force or military commitments, comparative case studies help to clarify the arguments and counterarguments related to these commitments. These case studies also examine the international and domestic political circumstances influencing U.S. foreign policy decisions. The cases presented in Chapter II of this volume include the period leading up to the U.S. involvement in the First World War, i.e.,1914–1917, followed by the renaissance of isolationism in the strict neutrality policy of the 1930s and early 1940s. The final case in Chapter II covers the period leading up to the entry of the United States into the Second World War. In these periods, as the case studies illustrate, U.S. foreign policy fluctuated between rigid neutrality and full-fledged military engagement.

---

[25] Jussi M. Hanhimäki, "Global Visions and Parochial Politics: The Persistent Dilemma of the 'American Century,'" *Diplomatic History* 27, no. 4 (2003): 446, ProQuest (60671679).

[26] Ibid., 427.

The postwar period and the era of détente is examined in detail in Chapter III of this book. With the end of the Second World War, the Truman-Kennan Containment Policy (1947) set the course for foreign policy for the years to come, acknowledging the United States could not reject its leading role in the international system. The postwar debates, however, presumed that the United States might again adopt a policy of reluctant engagement toward Europe. The communist threat of 1947–1948 and the weakness of the European democracies rendered the international security environment vulnerable. With the formation of NATO, the debate about U.S. military contributions to Europe finally ended with the recognition that U.S. interests depended on its participation in the alliance.

In the era of détente from the mid-1960s to the mid-1970s, the Mansfield Resolutions called for a reduction of U.S. troops in Europe. U.S. engagement in Europe under the Soviet threat at the height of the Cold War went largely unquestioned. As that threat abated and U.S. public support for the Indochina war waned, discussions to reduce military contributions to European security gained traction. Thus, the Mansfield case provides insight into the attempts to reduce U.S. troops in Europe and delivers counterarguments to the prevailing view about U.S. commitments to European security in the periods leading up to the world wars.

The conclusion of this work summarizes the findings from the case studies examined in Chapters II and III and evaluates whether the findings prove the three hypotheses presented in this chapter. The second part of Chapter IV applies these findings to the contemporary debate about the Trump administration's foreign policy toward Europe and NATO. Due to Trump's tumultuous start in the first few months of 2017, in which his commitment to the alliance underwent some adjustments, this volume represents the situation as of April 15, 2017.

II. THE CHALLENGES OF THE TWO WORLD WARS

The First and Second World Wars caused a huge turmoil in the international system. America's isolationism in the 1890s ended when the country could no longer ignore the negative effects of this policy on its security. The conduct of foreign policy from extreme neutrality toward full-fledged engagement revealed the country's resentments toward accepting a greater role in European and global security. Finally, the United States had no other choice than to enter the First World War and defeat the aggressors. In the aftermath of the First World War, the pendulum of foreign policy and public opinion had swung fully toward isolationism, where it remained fixed. Thus, in the periods leading up to each war, the administration had to overcome strong resistance and convince the U.S. public from going to war. The following sections analyze the political implications of and the obstacles stalling U.S. involvement in the wars in Europe. Each case starts with a brief summary of the whole period to provide the reader an overview, followed by an in-depth analysis in chronological order.

A. The Path to the First World War and its Aftermath

The First World War marks a transition in the U.S. position on and in international affairs. This transformation also manifested in some of the leading personalities of the time, including most prominently Woodrow Wilson. The road to interventionism was neither clear nor easy; however, the immediate aftermath of the war seemed to have consigned the Wilsonian experiment with collective security and global norms to the ranks of a fleeting fashion. In any event, it set the stage for American involvement in the world—just as it set the tone for the debates that attend this intervention.

1. Historical Overview

As war erupted in Europe in the summer of 1914, America's customs of non-entanglement in European great power politics since the late 18th century became the center of a debate about how the United

States should respond to the Great War in Europe. Herring explains that by 1914 the United States adhered to the tradition of neutrality outlined in the Farewell Address and the Monroe Doctrine.[27] The nation adhered to this position at first for domestic policy reasons, because of economic bonds with the conflict parties, and due to the remoteness of the American continent. Arthur Stanley Link writes that the U-boat war with the sinking of the Lusitania in May 1915 triggered a neutrality crisis in the years 1915–1916.[28] With the election in 1916, according to Link, Wilson adopted a more internationalist position, developed the idea of a new world order, and strictly urged for a compromise peace.[29]

The policy of neutrality ended in the spring of 1917 with the U.S. realization that such isolation had reached a dead end. Herring explains that the signals coup of the Zimmerman telegram (detailed later in this chapter), calling for a Mexican offensive, and the revival of the unrestricted U-boat war in April 1917 pulled the United States into war.[30] Wilson hoped the war would be for a Kantian new world order based on collective security, and he hoped this new world order would be led by the United States' superior role within the Western civilizations rather than the old diplomacy of a discredited Europe.[31] His new internationalism and collective security, however, did not endure much beyond 1920, when the U.S. Senate rejected membership in the League of Nations. In the 1920s, according to Herring, U.S. statecraft was one of prosperity and commerce, as well as consumer efficiency, but also the outlawing of war and arms control, all of which ended poorly in the new decade.[32]

---

[27] Herring, *From Colony to Superpower*, 399–402.
[28] Arthur Stanley Link, *Wilson: The Struggle for Neutrality 1914–15* (Princeton, NJ: Princeton University Press, 1960), 372–73.
[29] Arthur Stanley Link, *Wilson: Campaigns for Progressivism and Peace 1916–17* (Princeton, NJ: Princeton University Press, 1965), ix.
[30] Herring, *From Colony to Superpower*, 409.
[31] Ibid., 411.
[32] Ibid., 436.

2. November 1912 to June 1914—Preludes to War

In the 1912 presidential election, Democratic presidential candidate Woodrow Wilson benefited from the unusual fact that the Republican Party had nominated two candidates. According to historian Jean-Baptiste Duroselle, President Taft ran for the official Republican Party, whereas former President Theodore Roosevelt represented the progressive part of the party.[33] Although the majority of the voters were clearly Republican, the split of the Republican Party finally brought Wilson an overwhelming victory: Wilson gained 435 electoral votes; Roosevelt, 88; and Taft, 8.[34] After he lost the election, Roosevelt was a strong opponent of Wilson's policy.

Four political peers decisively influenced Wilson's policy—Edward Mandel House, Louis D. Brandeis, William J. Bryan, and Robert Lansing. Link explains that House and Wilson had a close friendship, and House became Wilson's closest aide and most influential advisor on European politics, although he did not hold office.[35] According to Walker, House believed that a close relationship with Britain and the stability of the European balance of power system was essential for American and European security.[36]

Brandeis, according to Link, was a strong supporter of free enterprise for small businesses and convinced Wilson to reform the tariff and banking system and curb the power of big business.[37] When Wilson came to power, as Herring explains, he was willing "to restore equality of opportunity and democracy" and make economic freedom an integral part of America's way of life—the New Freedom reform program.[38]

---

[33] Duroselle, *From Wilson to Roosevelt*, 24.

[34] Ibid.

[35] Arthur Stanley Link, *Woodrow Wilson and the Progressive Era 1910–1917* (New York: Harper & Brothers, 1954), 26.

[36] Douglas Earl Walker, "The Phoenix of Foreign Policy: Isolationism's Influence on U.S. Foreign Policy during the Twentieth Century" (master's thesis, Naval Postgraduate School, 1992), 23.

[37] Link, *Woodrow Wilson and the Progressive Era*, 20.

[38] Herring, *From Colony to Superpower*, 380.

Bryan, as Link asserts, had supported Wilson during the election campaign and was rewarded with a position as the head of the State Department.[39] According to Duroselle, Bryan was a strong believer in pacifism and Christian values; he was convinced that all wars were wrong, and that contention could be avoided through treaties.[40] Bryan later broke with Wilson over taking a too belligerent position toward Germany on the verge of the war. Lansing replaced him as the new Secretary of State in 1915 and stayed in office until 1920 when he also fell out of Wilson's favor because of a dispute about the importance of the League of Nations.

Wilson himself, as Herring explains, had little experience in foreign policy;[41] in fact, as Duroselle notes, before 1913, Wilson interested himself in foreign policy only when the issue at hand had an underlying domestic connection.[42] Still, Wilson held certain moral principles that were based on his Presbyterian background,[43] and he brought a firm religious conviction about America's exceptional status into statecraft; the nation should "show other peoples 'how they shall walk in the path of liberty.'"[44] In other words, as Link explains, Wilson was dedicated to democratic ideals and obsessed with a missionary foreign policy.[45] According to Duroselle, the president thought in terms of the equality of nations, humanity, and the Kantian "Plan for Perpetual Peace"; thus, he wanted to make "the world safe for democracy,'" emphasizing the "'necessity of an international organization.'"[46] Consequently, Wilson subordinated material interests to moral principles and believed "that man was sufficiently good so that democracy was the most humane and most Christian form of government."[47] So, Wilson saw the mission of

---

[39] Link, *Woodrow Wilson and the Progressive Era*, 12-13, 26.
[40] Duroselle, *From Wilson to Roosevelt*, 32.
[41] Herring, *From Colony to Superpower*, 381.
[42] Duroselle, *From Wilson to Roosevelt*, 34.
[43] Ibid.
[44] Herring, *From Colony to Superpower*, 380.
[45] Link, *Woodrow Wilson and the Progressive Era*, 81.
[46] Duroselle, *From Wilson to Roosevelt*, 34.
[47] Ibid., 35.

the United States "to realize the ideal of liberty, to furnish a model of democracy, to defend moral principles," and because the "greatest victories have been victories of peace and humanity," the Americans should "lead the world."[48]

Soon after taking office, Wilson and Bryan applied their abstract principles to practical foreign policy. For instance, as Link explains, Wilson negotiated a treaty with Colombia by which he wanted to restore America's moral prestige and repair the damage of gunboat diplomacy practiced by former President Theodore Roosevelt.[49] This policy won sympathies from the Latin American countries but provoked the Republican opposition. Roosevelt, as Duroselle writes, "spoke of a 'crime against the United States' and 'an attack on the honor of the United States.'"[50]

The same moral standards primarily influenced Wilson's Open Door Policy in the Far East and Europe. In the case of China, as Link writes, Wilson opposed an international railroad consortium, which seemed to illegally create a regime in China and favored Chinese efforts for independence and self-government.[51] In Europe, in the years 1913 to 1914, according to Herring, Wilson and Bryan sought to negotiate peace by a series of bilateral treaties with 20 nations to prevent the outbreak of a military conflict.[52] These so-called Bryan Treaties set the basis for later proposals of a League of Nations and marked the beginning of an U.S. internationalist foreign policy. However, despite these efforts, Wilson's diplomacy could not prevent the outbreak of the First World War.

---

[48] Duroselle, *From Wilson to Roosevelt*, 35.

[49] Link, *Woodrow Wilson and the Progressive Era*, 104.

[50] Duroselle, *From Wilson to Roosevelt*, 37.

[51] Link, *Woodrow Wilson and the Progressive Era*, 83–84.

[52] Herring, *From Colony to Superpower*, 382.

3. June 1914 to April 1917—American Neutrality and Entering the War

The outbreak of the European War shocked the Americans but did not really concern them, either because of the nation's general principle of neutrality or because of the U.S. lack of interest in European affairs. Bailey explains that when Archduke Francis Ferdinand was shot in Sarajevo on June 28, 1914, the Americans ignored the significance of this event, remained fundamentally isolationist, and refused to "plunge into the European blood bath."[53] According to Duroselle, the long tradition of non-involvement in European affairs, which manifested in the Monroe Doctrine,[54] accompanied a view that American interests had not been at stake since; furthermore, the European War "had nothing of a crusade of good against evil," and the Americans little admired the Entente camp.[55] Bailey asserts that Americans of German, Irish, Italian, and British origin sympathized with one or the other European adversary, which made Wilson anxious about damaging the fragile American immigrant society by favoring one side.[56] Neutrality was the obvious choice.

Nonetheless, neutrality did not mean non-involvement. Bailey points out that Wilson repeatedly insisted in public that the United States absolutely had "'no part in making' the war."[57] On the other hand, according to Herring, the president saw the war as an opportunity to establish a new world order.[58] Wilson did not desist from his peace mission. For instance, according to Duroselle, House negotiated naval disarmament with Germany, France, and Britain from May to July 1914 shortly before the outbreak of the war; however, the Sarajevo shooting overshadowed the trip, and the diplomatic efforts to preserve Europe

---

[53] Bailey, *Woodrow Wilson & The Lost Peace*, 2.
[54] For further details, see Appendix.
[55] Duroselle, *From Wilson to Roosevelt*, 40.
[56] Bailey, *Woodrow Wilson & The Lost Peace*, 2.
[57] Ibid., 3.
[58] Herring, *From Colony to Superpower*, 399.

from stumbling into war failed.[59] Neutrality now permitted Wilson to mediate between the conflict parties.

U.S. emergence as a growing power made neutrality a critical endeavor. Herring explains that the emotional and cultural background limited Wilson and his advisors' impartiality and, except for Bryan, most favored the Allies.[60] U.S. military power gave the country a decisive role in the conflict, but economic ties to Europe, especially with the Allies, also became important for the outcome of the war. Still suffering from an economic downturn, the United States viewed trade neutrality as unacceptable.[61]

On August 20, 1914, according to Link, the British imposed a sea blockade on Germany, denying access to strategic raw materials, in order to strangle Germany economically and to prevent neutral shipping from entering European ports.[62] Duroselle writes that, in November 1914, Britain declared the North Sea a theater of war and in March 1915 finally prohibited all neutral commerce with Germany.[63] Although faced with political headwind from German and Irish interest groups in the United States, merchants, munitions sellers, and agricultural producers, Wilson decided to acquiesce to Britain's blockade policy because, as Herring writes, "U.S. trade with Germany was not important enough to make a fuss over."[64] The United States did not want a conflict with Britain.

The German U-boat war changed U.S. policy. Germany's answer to the British blockade was a submarine campaign around the British Isles beginning in February 1915 that also affected neutral shipping. This time, according to Herring, Wilson took a firm stand against Germany's policy, holding the Germans accountable for any damage to U.S. citizens and vessels.[65] The test came on May 7, 1915, when a German

---

[59] Duroselle, *From Wilson to Roosevelt*, 41–42.

[60] Herring, *From Colony to Superpower*, 400.

[61] Ibid.

[62] Link, *Wilson: Struggle for Neutrality*, 107.

[63] Duroselle, *From Wilson to Roosevelt*, 43.

[64] Herring, *From Colony to Superpower*, 401.

[65] Ibid., 402.

torpedo sank the British luxury liner *Lusitania*, which caused the death of 128 U.S. citizens. According to Link, the *Lusitania* incident had a jolting effect on the American public and it marked the dividing line between previously unorganized calls for U.S. participation and substantial interventionist pressure.[66] Actually, the public wanted the president to express moral indignation but to avoid involvement in the war and applauded when he announced that "There is such a thing as a man being too proud to fight."[67] Exasperated by the incident, the Republican opposition under former President Roosevelt, on the other hand, thirsted for war and classified Wilson a "flapdoodle pacifist."[68] In sum, the *Lusitania* case finally brought the war to the United States.

The reaction of the U.S. government was threefold. Duroselle explains that House, who was on his second diplomatic peace mission in Europe, cabled from London that the United States could no longer remain neutral.[69] Pacifist Secretary of State Bryan, according to Link, suggested simultaneously protesting against Germany's U-boat war and Britain's blockade. Along with other members of the cabinet, he emphasized that U.S. citizens should avoid traveling on ships of the belligerent parties.[70] Wilson took a middle course since the public still was not ready to go to war. Duroselle explains that the president authorized the use of force if Germany continued sinking ships, but he did not prohibit traveling on belligerent ships.[71] Since Wilson had rejected Bryan's pacifist and isolationist advice, the secretary resigned on June 8, 1915, Link writes.[72] When Lansing replaced Bryan, a dissenting voice disappeared from the Cabinet.

In spring and summer 1916, the United States was in a neutrality crisis when the tensions with Germany increased. Herring explains that Germany accepted Wilson's proposal and promised to recognize the

---

[66] Link, *Wilson: Struggle for Neutrality*, 372–73.
[67] Quoted in Link, *Woodrow Wilson and the Progressive Era*, 165.
[68] Bailey, *Woodrow Wilson & The Lost Peace*, 4.
[69] Duroselle, *From Wilson to Roosevelt*, 46.
[70] Link, *Wilson: Struggle for Neutrality*, 384.
[71] Duroselle, *From Wilson to Roosevelt*, 46.
[72] Link, *Woodrow Wilson and the Progressive Era*, 166.

freedom of the seas.⁷³ This accord initially seemed to be stable. Even after the sinking of the British liner *The Arabic* on August 19, 1916, which killed two Americans, Wilson did not think in terms of war, according to Link.⁷⁴

On March 24, 1916, a German U-boat torpedoed the French cross channel ferry *Sussex*, killing 80 passengers and injuring four U.S. citizens. According to Bailey, the exasperated president presented an ultimatum to Berlin to stop the submarine warfare; otherwise, he would break diplomatic relations.⁷⁵ Furthermore, as Duroselle points out, a diplomatic crisis occurred in late 1915, when the Unites States discovered that the German military and naval attachés von Papen and Boy-Ed were involved in sabotage plans against factories and bridges, which culminated in the Black Tom explosion; furthermore, German ambassador Graf von Bernstorff threatened to influence German-Americans in the upcoming presidential election.⁷⁶ Germany had gone too far.

Meanwhile the tensions with Britain also increased. According to John Ravenhill, in 1913, cotton was the single most important export for the United States.⁷⁷ When Britain declared cotton contraband, as Herring explains, the United Kingdom averted an economic conflict with the United States only because it bought enough U.S. cotton to stabilize the prices.⁷⁸ Then, as Link writes, the brutal suppression of the Easter Revolution in Ireland on April 24, 1916, followed by a series of executions, made the Irish-Americans furious and alienated many other people who had been sympathetic to Britain.⁷⁹ Furthermore, in summer 1916, according to Duroselle, the British tightened restrictions on the high seas and blacklisted 87 U.S. firms and 350 Latin businesses for trading with the Central Powers. This move encouraged Wilson to

---

⁷³ Herring, *From Colony to Superpower*, 404.

⁷⁴ Link, *Woodrow Wilson and the Progressive Era*, 168.

⁷⁵ Bailey, *Woodrow Wilson & The Lost Peace*, 5.

⁷⁶ Duroselle, *From Wilson to Roosevelt*, 48.

⁷⁷ John Ravenhill, *Global Political Economy*, 4th ed. (Oxford, UK: Oxford University Press, 2014), 9.

⁷⁸ Herring, *From Colony to Superpower*, 404.

⁷⁹ Link, *Woodrow Wilson and the Progressive Era*, 218.

warn the British that the United States would take a firm position with London unless it retracted the blacklist, but the British refused.[80] Meanwhile, House was on his third diplomatic mission to Europe to offer mediation to the belligerent parties, but, as Link points out, the British and French leaders were unwilling to accept U.S. help unless the situation was so desperate that they were losing the war.[81] The parties did not accept an American mediation.

In 1915–1916, the political discourse focused on the question of U.S. military preparedness for potential conflicts. According to Link, the *Lusitania* incident sparked the preparedness movement, which was supported by various defense societies with close ties to the Republican Party and the military and financial complex.[82] On the other hand, as Herring explains, a progressive anti-preparedness movement had strong support in the South and Middle West, and activists blamed bankers and munition-makers for fostering the war because of economic interests.[83] Internationalists believed that only active and permanent involvement in world politics could preserve the American way of life, whereas progressivists insisted that only peace could ensure the domestic advancement of Roosevelt's New Nationalism.[84] Anti-preparedness progressivism gave rise to a new wave of isolationism that saw the country's "long-standing tradition of non-involvement [in European affairs] as a way of safeguarding the nation's way of life," Herring writes.[85] The idea of non-involvement in Europe grew strong among the U.S. public.

In addition to all its diplomatic efforts, the Wilson administration had taken certain precautionary measures to increase military and naval "preparedness." With the outbreak of the war, as Duroselle describes, Wilson first refused to reinforce the army because he "believed more

---

[80] Duroselle, *From Wilson to Roosevelt*, 51.
[81] Link, *Woodrow Wilson and the Progressive Era*, 220.
[82] Ibid., 179.
[83] Herring, *From Colony to Superpower*, 405.
[84] Ibid., 406; The central argument of Roosevelt's New Nationalism was the protection of human welfare and property rights by a powerful federal government.
[85] Ibid., 407.

in moral declarations than in arms."[86] In March 1915, Wilson accepted an increase of the Navy and, under the impact of the *Lusitania* incident, in June 1915, he finally asked Secretary of War Lindley Miller Garrison to elaborate plans for a significant increase of the Army to 1,500,000 men.[87] Link explains that the naval improvement program aimed to achieve equality with the British navy by 1925, which required an investment of $500 million.[88] The United States was on the way to becoming a military world power although thoughts about an intervention in Europe were still far away.

The 1916 presidential election campaign fell in the middle of the neutrality crisis, and the failure of House's diplomatic mission had dashed Wilson's ambitions for the election. Duroselle writes that the Democratic Party was divided since it included many pacifists and Wilson's military preparedness measures were not popular.[89] Hence, as Link writes, Bryan led the campaign, in which peace and social justice became central themes.[90] As a result, Wilson focused more on domestic policy affairs, adopted Roosevelt's New Nationalism, and henceforth fought for better working conditions, social justice, and women's rights.

Although the focus of the campaign was on domestic affairs, the election was largely about foreign policy. According to Duroselle, the Republican Party chose Charles Evans Hughes as its candidate because Roosevelt had declared his support of the European war and the potential for American involvement was still unpopular.[91] Wilson, however, accused the Republicans of favoring the war, and, as Link writes, the slogan "He Kept Us Out of War" was a central element of his campaign.[92] Furthermore, as Herring explains, Wilson formulated a new internationalist concept that would allow the United States to gain a

---

[86] Duroselle, *From Wilson to Roosevelt*, 57.

[87] Ibid.

[88] Link, *Woodrow Wilson and the Progressive Era*, 179.

[89] Duroselle, *From Wilson to Roosevelt*, 51.

[90] Link, *Woodrow Wilson and the Progressive Era*, 243.

[91] Duroselle, *From Wilson to Roosevelt*, 52.

[92] Link, *Woodrow Wilson and the Progressive Era*, 242.

leadership position in the world—the Americans "have got to serve the world."[93] Wilson won the election narrowly.

The reelection encouraged the president to strengthen his international course. Since the president was in fear of the United States being dragged into the war, he undertook a new diplomatic attempt to end the European conflict but failed. On December 18, 1916, as Link points out, Wilson invited the belligerent parties to negotiate a peace settlement and define their war objectives.[94] According to Herring, in January 1917, the president sketched out a "covenant of cooperative peace" as a proposal to the U.S. Senate, in which the United States should play a key role in the postwar settlement.[95] Herring further asserts that Wilson's proposal outraged Paris and London since, exhausted from the losses, their attitudes toward a peaceful solution were hardened.[96] None of the belligerents was willing to accept Wilson's proposal.

Most Americans still did not want war but were soon jarred out of their daydreams. On January 31, 1917, as Link writes, Germany announced a policy of unrestricted submarine warfare, which led the president to break diplomatic relations with Germany on February 3, 1917.[97] Although severing diplomatic relations usually meant going to war, Wilson still did not believe that a war was coming. Bailey asserts that the president wanted to wait until overt hostilities occurred, especially since the U.S. public did not understand the full significance of the events and wanted the administration not to lead "the nation into the bloody abyss."[98]

Within a month this attitude changed. Duroselle explains that the British had captured and deciphered a note sent by German Foreign Secretary Arthur Zimmermann on January 19, 1916, which offered Mexico an alliance with Germany in return for reconquering the former

---

[93] Herring, *From Colony to Superpower*, 407.
[94] Link, *Woodrow Wilson and the Progressive Era*, 261.
[95] Herring, *From Colony to Superpower*, 408.
[96] Ibid.
[97] Link, *Wilson: Campaigns for Progressivism and Peace*, 290, 298.
[98] Bailey, *Woodrow Wilson & The Lost Peace*, 6-7.

Mexican territories of Texas, New Mexico, and Arizona; furthermore, Mexico should invite Japan to support the invasion.[99] Link asserts that the capture of the Zimmerman telegram now revealed a direct threat to the country, which exasperated the Americans and convinced them of Germany's hostile intentions.[100] The United States took a huge step toward war.

In addition to these diplomatic offences, the U-boat war had severe economic effects, and the desire for freedom of commerce forced the United States into war. Bailey explains that, since American vessels were afraid of entering the war zone, supplies were piling up in American ports and did not reach the Allies on the European battlefield, which caused an economic paralysis that the country could no longer endure. The situation encouraged Wilson to ask the Congress for the authority to arm the merchant ships.[101] Despite these arming measures, according to Duroselle, five vessels were sunk by mid-March.[102] The Germans were forcing America into war.

Wilson had no other alternative but to ask Congress on April 2, 1917, for a declaration of war, which, according to Bailey, the two houses granted with an overwhelming majority on April 4 and 6.[103] In his war message to Congress Wilson said,

> The present German submarine warfare against commerce is a warfare against mankind. It is a war against all nations. ... I thought that it would suffice to assert our neutral rights with arms, our right to use the seas against unlawful interference, our right to keep our people safe against unlawful violence. But armed neutrality, it now appears, is impracticable. ... We desire no conquest, no dominion. We seek no indemnities for ourselves, no material compensation for the sacrifices we shall freely make. We are but one of the champions

---

[99] Duroselle, *From Wilson to Roosevelt*, 67.
[100] Link, *Woodrow Wilson and the Progressive Era*, 273.
[101] Bailey, *Woodrow Wilson & The Lost Peace*, 8.
[102] Duroselle, *From Wilson to Roosevelt*, 68.
[103] Bailey, *Woodrow Wilson & The Lost Peace*, 10.

of the rights of mankind. We shall be satisfied when those rights have been made as secure as the faith and the freedom of nations can make them. ...We shall fight for the things which we have always carried nearest our hearts, for democracy, for the right of those who submit to authority to have a voice in their own Governments, for the rights and liberties of small nations, for a universal dominion of right by such a concert of free peoples as shall bring peace and safety to all nations and make the world itself at last free.[104]

In sum, Wilson's primary argument was the freedom of commerce, which he, according to Duroselle, immediately intertwined with his personal "crusade for democracy" and "his well-developed ideology and his vision of the future."[105] Wilson hereby followed a pragmatic approach because "when the public was opposed to a decision, ... it must be educated."[106]

On the other hand, when the United States declared war, there was no sign that the Allies might lose. Thus, the sole cause of war was the principle of freedom of the seas. Instead of promoting democracy, the United States wanted to make "the world safe against the submarine," Bailey asserts.[107] Actually, Wilson combined the immediate economic cause with some more compelling missionary objectives to arouse the people from their apathy. According to Bailey, the president had, however, forgotten to consider the broad isolationist sentiment and ignored those "who were willing to leave the Allies in the lurch" once the U-boat war was won.[108] Wilson refused to acknowledge that he might be overpowered by public opinion.

---

[104] Woodrow Wilson, "President Wilson's Declaration of War Message to Congress," 100 Milestone Documents, U.S. National Archives and Records Administration, April 2, 1917, https://www.ourdocuments.gov/doc.php?doc=62&page=transcript.

[105] Duroselle, *From Wilson to Roosevelt*, 69–70.

[106] Ibid., 70.

[107] Bailey, *Woodrow Wilson & The Lost Peace*, 13–15.

[108] Ibid.

4. April 1917 to October 1918—Wilson's Ideas for a New Internationalism

Wilson's ideas for a stable peace and a new world order were born long before the war ended. The president molded his Kantian worldview into a peace program that he presented during a joint session of Congress on January 8, 1918.[109] Out of his Fourteen Points, points VI to XIII cover territorial issues among the belligerent parties, but points I to V and point XIV include general principles for a stable peace. Wilson urges for "open covenants for peace," freedom of the seas, the removal of "all economic barriers" and the establishment of free trade, reduction of national armaments, "adjustment of all colonial claims," and "a general association of nations" to guarantee "political independence and territorial integrity."[110] In other words, economic issues drove Wilson's policy, and the United States fought for its own interests.

With point XIV, the president proposed what would later become the League of Nations. Duroselle concludes that "the United States increasingly appeared to be the potential arbiter between nations."[111] According to Herring, this new "Wilsonianism" influenced U.S. foreign policy and world affairs for coming years because the president broke with the country's tradition of non-involvement in European politics.[112] By the summer of 1918, more than a million U.S. troops entered the European battlefields, which significantly changed the course of the war.

The American people, however, did not support Wilson's new diplomacy. Baily explains that during a speech in New York in September 1918, the president "spoke over the heads of the audience," and the most unimportant points caused the greatest applause; the Americans

---

[109] Woodrow Wilson, "President Woodrow Wilson's 14 Points," 100 Milestone Documents, U.S. National Archives and Records Administration, January 8, 1918, https://www.ourdocuments.gov/doc.php?doc=62&page=transcript.

[110] Ibid.

[111] Duroselle, *From Wilson to Roosevelt*, 79.

[112] Herring, *From Colony to Superpower*, 411-12.

had greater interest in "dethroning the Kaiser than in enthroning Wilsonian idealism."[113] Especially the Republicans did not follow Wilson's ideas of a new world order and lowering trade barriers. Bailey further writes that the president's opponents called the Fourteen Points "the 'fourteen commandments' of 'God Almighty Wilson.'"[114] Open opposition, however, did not come to the surface until the war ended. Furthermore, as Herring asserts, Wilson's points were too vague and illusory to make them a good basis for a future peace.[115] Even under the best circumstances, Wilson could not fully realize his plans.

Because of the vagueness of Wilson's plans, unsurprisingly, every party interpreted the president's plan in its own favor. According to Bailey, the president was so convinced by his plans that he dropped more than 60 million leaflets in Latin America, the Far East, and Europe advertising his vision of a new world order.[116] Initially, the Germans first saw the Fourteen Points as an effrontery because they had won most of the battles in early 1918; later, however, as Duroselle writes, the Fourteen Points became a central argument to attenuate the armistice.[117] The European allies, on the other hand, were not willing to give up their booty after years of a bloody war. Although the Allied governments stayed calm since they needed U.S. support, Wilson's ideas were clearly not their vision of a European future, Bailey asserts.[118] The U.S. public, on the other hand, took Wilson's words too literally and accused the president of breaking faith and not insisting on his declared war aims.[119] The parties needed a few more months until they made further steps toward peace.

---

[113] Bailey, *Woodrow Wilson & The Lost Peace*, 24.

[114] Ibid., 25.

[115] Herring, *From Colony to Superpower*, 417.

[116] Bailey, *Woodrow Wilson & The Lost Peace*, 27.

[117] Duroselle, *From Wilson to Roosevelt*, 85.

[118] Bailey, *Woodrow Wilson & The Lost Peace*, 31.

[119] Ibid., 32–33.

5. October 1918 to March 1920—Messy Peace and the Defeat of Wilsonianism

Negotiations over an armistice revealed Wilson's delicate position. On October 6, 1918, Germany and Austria-Hungary directly approached the United States for an opening of armistice negotiations based on the Fourteen Points. Duroselle points out that Germany and Austria-Hungary both wanted to avoid severe punishment by the Entente and hoped for the United States to act as a mediator between the belligerents.[120] Historian Lloyd E. Ambrosius writes that the U.S. answer was clear: Germany should unconditionally accept the Fourteen Points.[121] Additionally, according to Duroselle, the United States insisted on negotiating peace only with a government that represented the German people and "not the military masters and the monarchical autocrats"; Germany accepted the conditions in their entirety on October 20, 1918, and House went to Europe to negotiate the peace.[122] Finally, the United States was in the mediator role that it had sought before.

The Allies were hesitant for various reasons, but House was finally able to secure acceptance with the reservation of the British. Specifically, Herring writes, Britain reserved the right to interpret freedom of the seas and required that Germany had to compensate the Allied powers for their civilian and property losses.[123] This was a triumph for Wilson. Nevertheless, the pre-armistice contract, according to Bailey, opened the way to serious problems since each of the parties still read the Fourteen Points in the light of their own expectations.[124]

Ambrosius explains that the U.S. public was not convinced of Wilson's policy and favored unconditional surrender—especially the Republicans—who argued that negotiation meant losing the war.[125] From

---

[120] Duroselle, *From Wilson to Roosevelt*, 85.

[121] Lloyd E. Ambrosius, *Woodrow Wilson and the American Diplomatic Tradition: The Treaty Fight in Perspective* (New York, Cambridge University Press, 1987), 48.

[122] Duroselle, *From Wilson to Roosevelt*, 85–86.

[123] Herring, *From Colony to Superpower*, 417.

[124] Bailey, *Woodrow Wilson & The Lost Peace*, 46–47.

[125] Ambrosius, *Woodrow Wilson and the American Diplomatic Tradition*, 49.

within the senate, according to Bailey, there were even threats of impeaching the president for catering to the Germans.[126] Wilson's unpopular policy, according to Herring, would later hamper his ability to negotiate peace and sell the League of Nations concept to the American people.[127] Regardless of possible consequences, the president carried on with his course of ending the war as quickly as possible, but he did not take the U.S. voters into account.

The mid-term congressional elections became the final blow to Wilson's internationalism. According to Bailey, the Republicans had supported the war but opposed the administration, which was appealing to the electorate, and since the Democrats controlled the Senate only by a small margin, Democratic congressmen urged Wilson to ask the people to vote for the Democrats.[128] Wilson promised help, and on October 25, 1918, he released a message to the press where he stressed possible foreign reactions to the vote. He said,

> If you have approved of my leadership and wish me to continue to be your unembarrassed spokesman in affairs at home and abroad, I earnestly beg that you will express yourself unmistakably to that effect by returning a Democratic majority to both the Senate and the House of Representatives. ... The return of a Republican majority to either House of the Congress would, moreover, certainly be interpreted on the other side of the water as a repudiation of my leadership.[129]

The message, however, was a big political mistake. Wilson had turned the election into a vote of confidence for his policy toward Europe, and it violated the political truce. Although the Republicans had loyally supported the war, now they were declared untrustworthy to

---

[126] Bailey, *Woodrow Wilson & The Lost Peace*, 40.

[127] Herring, *From Colony to Superpower*, 416.

[128] Bailey, *Woodrow Wilson & The Lost Peace*, 58–59.

[129] Woodrow Wilson, "Statement Appealing to the Nation for Support in the 1918 Congressional Election," American Presidency Project, October 25, 1918, http://www.presidency.ucsb.edu/ws/?pid=110491.

make the peace. According to Bailey, "a Republican roar of anger reverberated from coast to coast."[130] Wilson's interference into the campaign set free a now-or-never mentality, which, as historian Thomas J. Knock writes, caused "a great political defeat at home" that gave the Republicans a moderate majority.[131] Bailey points out that the election united the discordant factions within the Republican Party and focused their aims toward the presidential elections in 1920: now, "Wilson and his works must be defeated at all costs."[132]

Unabashed, Wilson carried on with his peace policy. After the abdication of the German Emperor Wilhelm II and the signing of the armistice on November 11, 1918, Wilson said in an address to the American people: "Everything for which America fought has been accomplished. It will now be our fortunate duty to assist by example, by sober and friendly council and material aid in the establishment of a just democracy throughout the world."[133] Wilson insisted on his idealistic vision of a new world order and, according to Ambrosius, "anticipated the fulfillment of this missionary task in Paris."[134] Critics on both sides of the Atlantic, as Bailey explains, claimed that Wilson, having lost the support of the U.S. voters during the mid-term election, no longer had the legitimacy to negotiate the peace.[135] Wilson, however, wanted to lead the U.S. peace delegation.

The peace conference opened on January 12, 1919, and Wilson remained abroad for more than six months. Duroselle writes that, among the delegation of 1,300 experts, Secretary of State Lansing and House accompanied the president.[136] Since foreign policy now was his dominant agenda, Wilson personally conducted major negotiations, taking the chance to transform his vision of a peaceful world order into the

---

[130] Bailey, *Woodrow Wilson & The Lost Peace*, 60.

[131] Thomas J. Knock, *To End All Wars: Woodrow Wilson and the Quest for a New World Order* (New York: Oxford University Press, 1992), 184.

[132] Bailey, *Woodrow Wilson & The Lost Peace*, 62–63.

[133] Quoted in Duroselle, *From Wilson to Roosevelt*, 87.

[134] Ambrosius, *Woodrow Wilson and the American Diplomatic Tradition*, 50.

[135] Bailey, *Woodrow Wilson & The Lost Peace*, 68.

[136] Duroselle, *From Wilson to Roosevelt*, 90–91.

League of Nations under Anglo-American leadership. Wilson explained, "There must now be not a balance of power, not a powerful group of nations set off against each other, but a single overwhelming, powerful group of nations who shall be the trustee of the peace of the world."[137] According to Herring, Wilson was so obsessed by his idea, believing that an effective League would mitigate all inequities and shortfalls in the peace agreement, that he even accepted issues of the peace treaty left unsettled.[138] Thereby, Wilson was able to secure an agreement to a League with an assembly that included all nations and a council of the five victorious powers plus four elected members.[139] At the end, however, there was not much left of the Fourteen Points, and "liberals across the world expressed shock and bitterness" about a peace settlement, which exasperated the Germans and disappointed colonial peoples, which had hopes for national self-determination.[140] Wilson had intertwined the peace treaty with his plans for the League and thereby left Europe with an insufficient treaty.

Furthermore, the Covenant of the League included highly controversial elements. Ambrosius writes that Wilson, with the help of the League, wanted to "revert to traditional isolation from the Old World" but also to project American influence throughout the world.[141] Most controversial, however, was Article X that included a collective security mechanism, which reads, "The Members of the League undertake to respect and preserve as against external aggression the territorial integrity and existing political independence of all Members of the League. In case of any such aggression … the Council shall advise upon the means by which this obligation shall be fulfilled."[142] Thus, the covenant combined internationalist and isolationist elements, which alarmed Wilson's opponents. For instance, as Knock writes, Theodore

---

[137] Quoted in Ambrosius, *Woodrow Wilson and the American Diplomatic Tradition*, 53.

[138] Herring, *From Colony to Superpower*, 423.

[139] Ibid.

[140] Ibid., 426.

[141] Ambrosius, *Woodrow Wilson and the American Diplomatic Tradition*, 79.

[142] "The Covenant of the League of Nations," Avalon Project, Yale Law School, December 1924, http://avalon.law.yale.edu/20th_century/leagcov.asp#art1.

Roosevelt argued that the United States could never again "completely withdraw into its shell," and he questioned whether America was willing to go to war "every time a Jugoslav wishes to slap a Czechoslav in the face."[143] Although Wilson, according to Herring, was aware of the limits of his work, he signed the Versailles Treaty on June 28, 1919 and, after his return, presented it to Congress on July 10, 1919.[144] The great debate over America's future role in the world began.

Wilson's plans saw stiff opposition. According to Duroselle, the Republican leader of the Senate, Henry Cabot Lodge, generally opposed any democratic attempts and personally disliked Wilson.[145] Duroselle further explains that, at the beginning, Lodge was not particularly opposed to the idea of the League, but Theodore Roosevelt had persuaded him that "under no circumstances ... [should] the United States agree to police the Old World" and that one should not abandon the Monroe Doctrine.[146] Lodge warned against transferring sovereignty to the League, which required him to weaken the obligations of Article X. Duroselle writes that, sensing crumbling public support, Lodge consumed six weeks with reading all 268 pages to the Committee of Foreign Relations and invited witnesses raising pleas against the treaty, among them Lansing who had broken with Wilson in Paris.[147] Moreover, the public opposed the treaty. According to Bailey, German-Americans claimed that the treaty was too harsh, Italians wanted more territory for their motherland, and Irish ethnic groups rejected the treaty since it did not address Irish independence.[148] Facing a possible defeat, Wilson needed to convince the American people of his idea.

Despite the president's personal engagement, the Senate voted against the covenant. Duroselle writes that Wilson decided to enhance pressure on the opposition by conducting a promotion tour through

---

[143] Knock, *To End All Wars*, 229.

[144] Herring, *From Colony to Superpower*, 426–27.

[145] Duroselle, *From Wilson to Roosevelt*, 113.

[146] Ibid.

[147] Ibid., 114.

[148] Thomas A. Bailey, *Woodrow Wilson & The Great Betrayal* (New York: Quadrangle, 1945), 24–26.

the country during which he appealed to the "Americans to accept the responsibilities of world leadership."[149] Meanwhile, as Herring explains, the Foreign Relations Committee submitted 45 amendments and four reservations, most significantly excluding the Monroe Doctrine from League jurisdiction and restricting obligations toward Article X of the covenant.[150] The country would not accept the deployment of troops or going to war for a foreign country's territorial integrity or political independence without approval of Congress.

Wilson, however, did not want to make any sort of compromise. Lansing, for instance, explained that "the President is with his back to the wall and means to go down rather than surrender."[151] Duroselle writes that, after a first defeat in Congress in November 1919, Wilson on December 14, 1919, publicly declared he would refuse all compromise, not knowing about the lack of public interest in the League.[152] On March 19, 1920, the Senate finally rejected the Versailles Peace Treaty and the League, and for the next 20 years, the United States was oftentimes only a bystander while a messy peace and a powerless League set the stage for a second, even bloodier war.

B. The Interwar Period and the Prelude to the Second World War

The years from 1920 to 1941 saw major changes in the conduct of U.S. statecraft toward Europe. After the First World War and the non-entanglement of the United States in the League of Nations, as Herring explains, the 1920s were characterized by the lack of an overarching foreign political vision and an emphasis on domestic economic interests, best described as "involvement without commitment."[153] Isolationist attitudes came to the forefront as a response to the Great Depression since America felt well protected by two large bodies of water

---

[149] Duroselle, *From Wilson to Roosevelt*, 114–18; Herring, *From Colony to Superpower*, 431.

[150] Herring, *From Colony to Superpower*, 432.

[151] Quoted in Ambrosius, *Woodrow Wilson and the American Diplomatic Tradition*, 207.

[152] Duroselle, *From Wilson to Roosevelt*, 124–25.

[153] Herring, *From Colony to Superpower*, 436.

in the West and the East. Rising fascism and Germany's presumable rise as a new superpower, however, revealed that the United States was vulnerable and affected by events abroad. President Franklin Delano Roosevelt (FDR) underwent a remarkable metamorphosis from international statesman to domestic-focused politician and back. He realized that he had to teach the Americans his new course of foreign policy. Sometimes even with questionable methods, he managed to overcome an isolationist legislature, aided the European powers in fighting Nazi Germany, and created the basis for the Cold War, emphasizing America's responsibility for the security of the Western hemisphere. It became clear that the key for U.S. security was Europe, and democratic values had to be defended abroad.

1. Historical Overview

Economic issues dominated the U.S. foreign policy of the 1920s. Herring explains that America's primary interest was economic success, which needed stability and peace to explore foreign markets.[154] Duroselle points out that economic prosperity created a confidence and a desire for peace, which led to a false optimism about the power of treaties to maintain peace—the Kellogg-Briand Pact (1928) that ruled out war as a means of policy is such an example.[155] The 1920s ended with an unprecedented economic crisis—the Great Depression, in which isolationism became the dominant theme of domestic politics for the years to come. A symptom of the 1930s was the public aversion to war. For instance, as Duroselle asserts, the Nye Committee investigation on arms manufacturers of 1934 concluded that the United States had wrongly been drawn into war by bankers, munition makers, and by insidious British propaganda.[156] In 1935, neutrality laws followed, ignoring the upcoming crisis in Europe and Asia.

Herring writes that, despite public resistance, the German annexation of the Sudetenland in Czechoslovakia (1938) slowly led to a policy of war preparations and support for France and Britain through arms

---

[154] Herring, *From Colony to Superpower*, 436.

[155] Duroselle, *From Wilson to Roosevelt*, 167.

[156] Ibid., 238–40.

sales despite the neutrality laws.[157] Germany's quick wins in 1940, however, left Britain standing alone in Europe, which caused fear and a feeling of vulnerability and finally changed the U.S. attitude toward war after June 1940.[158] The worldwide strategy of Plan Dog (November 1940), as political scientist Marc Trachtenberg explains, became the subject of consensus in U.S. domestic politics after December 7, 1941; the defense of the United States must be carried to Europe and Asia.[159] Public resistance against a U.S. entanglement in the war remained alive until the attack on Pearl Harbor on December 7, 1941, and the German declaration of war on the following day.[160] False hopes of being able to maintain neutrality ended abruptly.

2. April 1921 to February 1932—Economic Prosperity and False Security

After the defeat of the League of Nations and the Versailles Treaty in 1920–1921, the newly elected President Warren Gamaliel Harding confronted a pile of diplomatic shards. Duroselle writes that Secretary of State Charles Evans Hughes worked out a new peace agreement incorporating the articles of the Versailles Treaty without the paragraphs concerning the League; furthermore, he arranged bilateral peace treaties with Germany, Austria, and Hungary.[161] With the opposition in the Senate, a membership in the League of Nations was far out of range. On April 2, 1921, Harding explained, "There will be no betrayal in the deliberate expression of the American people ... the League Covenant can have no sanction by us."[162] According to historian Robert Hugh Ferrell, the United States instead sought for membership in the World Court, but isolationist anti-League forces in the senate managed to place a reservation in the U.S. proposal, which was unacceptable for

---

[157] Herring, *From Colony to Superpower*, 513–15.
[158] Ibid., 519–20.
[159] Marc Trachtenberg, *The Craft of International History: A Guide to Method* (Princeton, NJ: Princeton University Press, 2006), 118–19.
[160] Herring, *From Colony to Superpower*, 536.
[161] Duroselle, *From Wilson to Roosevelt*, 145.
[162] Quoted in Ibid.

the signatories of the Court protocol.[163] Any attempts toward the League proved incapable of realization.

Non-entanglement did not include financial issues. Herring points out that political leaders were convinced that the spread of liberal capitalism could create a stable peace order since "commerce was 'the life blood of modern civilization.'"[164] The United States needed to create new markets in Europe; meanwhile, the Americans wanted to maintain low taxes at home and protect the domestic market with high tariffs on European imports, which was not a promising economic policy.[165] Thus, Hughes sought to reduce the burden of German war reparations. According to Duroselle, the 1924 Dawes plan scaled back Germany's annual reparation payments, with increasing payments over time as its economy improved, and additionally it floated the market with private loans.[166] As a result, between 1922 and 1929, the United States floated Germany with loans worth billions of dollars and became the "bankers to the world."[167] In 1929, the Young Plan called for significant reductions in German war reparations, which would still be enough that the Allies, on the other hand, could use the payments to meet their war debt obligations toward the United States; furthermore, the supervision of German finances ended, and the last U.S. troops left the country.[168] In other words, the United States focused on economic means to create peace and stability, which would allow furthering U.S. commercial expansionism.

---

[163] Robert Hugh Ferrell, *Peace in Their Time: The Origins of the Kellogg-Briand Pact* (New Haven: Yale University Press, 1952), 44.

[164] Herring, *From Colony to Superpower*, 445.

[165] Ibid., 448.

[166] Duroselle, *From Wilson to Roosevelt*, 149; the Dawes plan is named after Chicago banker Charles G. Dawes, who received the Nobel Peace Prize in 1925 for his contribution to solve the reparation crisis. See also "The Dawes Plan, the Young Plan, German Reparations, and Inter-allied War Debts," Office of the Historian, United States Department of State, accessed March 8, 2017, https://history.state.gov/milestones/1921-1936/dawes. Hereafter cited as "Dawes and Young Plan."

[167] Duroselle, *From Wilson to Roosevelt*, 173.

[168] "Dawes Plan and Young Plan"; Herring, *From Colony to Superpower*, 481.

Besides the strong economic focus and within the given political limitations, the Harding and Coolidge administrations fought for world peace. Although the United States had an aversion to the League, as Herring states, it took leadership in promoting arms limitations, which became an integral part of its diplomatic and economic policy.[169] The high-water mark of the 1920s was the Kellogg-Briand Pact signed on August 27, 1928, which outlawed war as an instrument of policy. Ferrell writes that France had built up alliances against Germany and now sought a way to tie the United States into the system or at least guarantee U.S. neutrality.[170] According to Herring, the French Foreign Minister Aristide Briand received support for his pacific idea from a well-organized U.S. peace movement, which put pressure on the Coolidge administration to join the pact.[171] Instead, U.S. Secretary of State Frank B. Kellogg made a counterproposal for a multilateral treaty, which was finally joined by 15 nations, among them all the great European powers.[172]

However, the Kellogg-Briand Pact was a "dangerous illusion because it created an artificial sense of security with no shadow of effective guarantee," Duroselle asserts.[173] Consequently, Ferrell renders a devastating verdict about U.S. foreign policy of the 1920s. He writes, "[American diplomats] had to cope with a public opinion whose only virtue often was that it was public and opinionated. The strength, voice, and unintelligence of American public opinion ... forced the State Department into tortuous diplomatic maneuvering—necessitating ... a multilateral treaty against war."[174] The false sense of security would determine the conduct of foreign security for the next years.

---

[169] Herring, *From Colony to Superpower*, 452.

[170] Ferrell, *Origins of the Kellogg-Briand Pact*, 263.

[171] Herring, *From Colony to Superpower*, 477–78.

[172] Ibid., 478.

[173] Duroselle, *From Wilson to Roosevelt*, 181.

[174] Ferrell, *Origins of the Kellogg-Briand Pact*, 265.

3. February 1932 to May 1937—The Height of Isolationism

Party politics influenced the political course of the newly elected president. When FDR presented himself as a candidate at the Democratic National Convention in June 1932, the Great Depression was the dominating theme. According to Duroselle, FDR needed the support of the party's right wing under William Randolph Hearst. Hearst followed a strict isolationist position, strongly opposed a "policy of meddling in European conflicts and complications," and even asked for a strict repudiation of the League of Nations in the name of "America first."[175] To secure Hearst's support, FDR announced in a speech to New York State Grange on February 2, 1932, that "American participation in the League would not serve the highest purpose of the prevention of war. … The highest ideals of America demand that with strict adherence to the principles of Washington, we maintain our international freedom."[176] This major concession to the right-wing isolationists gained FDR the necessary support to become a candidate for the Democratic Party. Furthermore, as Duroselle points out, FDR even decided to exclude foreign policy issues from his campaign and instead entirely concentrate on domestic problems promoting social democracy and government regulations, which finally attracted the public and gained him a comfortable majority in the election.[177] In other words, at the start of FDR's presidency, party politics and the severe economic crisis had narrowed FDR's political focus to domestic problems and encouraged him to promote a neutral position in foreign political affairs.

With such a predetermined agenda, unsurprisingly, the revitalization of the domestic economy dominated U.S. policy toward Europe. Herring asserts that within the first three years of the economic crisis the U.S. gross national product dropped by 50 percent and unemployment rates climbed to 25 percent; furthermore, during the long interregnum

---

[175] Duroselle, *From Wilson to Roosevelt*, 226, 227.

[176] Franklin Delano Roosevelt, "Speech to New York State Grange," FDR Library's Digital Collections, University of Illinois, February 2, 1932, 552, http://www.fdrlibrary.marist.edu/_resources/images/msf/msf00470.

[177] Duroselle, *From Wilson to Roosevelt*, 224, 228–29.

until FDR's inauguration on March 4, 1933, a series of bank collapses destroyed the savings of millions of depositors, which accelerated the crisis.[178] As a result, FDR firmly believed that the causes of the depression were at the domestic level. Although he knew that a revitalization of international trade relations might contribute to the solution of the crisis, he primarily focused on domestic issues. For instance, in his inaugural address he explained that the United States was fighting a war against the economic crisis; thus, the country "shall spare no effort to restore world trade by international economic readjustment. The crisis at home, however, could not wait on that accomplishment."[179] In other words, FDR focused on domestic issues and pushed international relations to the side.

As a result, the field of world policy occupied only a small part of FDR's inaugural speech. For instance, the president proclaimed the concept of the "Good Neighbor." He said, "I would dedicate this Nation to the policy of the good neighbor—the neighbor who resolutely respects himself and, because he does so, respects the rights of others."[180] FDR's Good Neighbor concept, according to John Lamberton Harper, was based on the anti-European idea of the Monroe Doctrine and proclaimed a new doctrine of non-interference in the internal affairs of Latin America.[181] Thus, FDR adopted traditional isolationist ideas.

Beyond the Good Neighbor policy, FDR's inaugural speech did not contain any word about foreign policy or the relationship with Europe. Hence, as Herring explains, "foreign policy fell to the bottom of the national scale of priorities," which destroyed the nation's self-confidence and focused popular hatred against the outside world.[182] As a result, as Duroselle points out, by the mid-1930s, the public believed

---

[178] Herring, *From Colony to Superpower*, 486, 494.

[179] Franklin Delano Roosevelt, "Inaugural Address," American Presidency Project, University of California, March 4, 1933, http://www.presidency.ucsb.edu/ws/?pid=14473.

[180] Roosevelt, "Inaugural Address."

[181] John Lamberton Harper, *American Visions of Europe* (New York: Cambridge University Press, 1996), 56.

[182] Herring, *From Colony to Superpower*, 502.

that the European adventure during the First World War had been a fatal error, and that America should avoid repeating such mistakes in the future.[183] The United States completely turned its focus toward domestic problems, and entanglement with the old world became a taboo.

U.S. rejection of foreign involvement resulted in a series of decisions that even further isolated the nation on the international level. Herring asserts that foreign policy through the 1930s was an issue of the State Department under Secretary Cordell Hull since FDR focused on solving domestic problems.[184] FDR's predecessor Hoover had initiated a World Monetary and Economic conference, which should have taken place in June 1933, to mitigate the depression on the international level. Hull was to negotiate it, but FDR sabotaged the conference from the very beginning. For instance, on May 16, 1933, the president said, "The World Economic Conference ... must, in short, supplement individual domestic programs for economic recovery, by wise and considered international action."[185] Four days later, on May 20, 1933, he announced in a radio speech that international trade was negligible, and "the heart of the program for recovery ... should be domestic."[186] In sum, as Harper explains, FDR's nationalist sentiments prevailed. During the conference, the president torpedoed Hull's attempts to stabilize currencies by returning to the gold standard.[187] In his famous "Bombshell Message" on July 3, 1933, FDR rejected Hull's plans and expressed his will to solve the economic problem at home.[188] In sum, FDR destroyed the last remnant of international cooperation to solve the economic crisis and immersed himself in domestic policy issues.

---

[183] Duroselle, *From Wilson to Roosevelt*, 238.

[184] Herring, *From Colony to Superpower*, 493.

[185] Franklin Delano Roosevelt, "Appeal for World Peace by Disarmament and for Relief from Economic Chaos," American Presidency Project, University of California, May 16, 1933, http://www.presidency.ucsb.edu/ws/index.php?pid=14643.

[186] Quoted in Duroselle, *From Wilson to Roosevelt*, 232.

[187] Harper, *American Visions of Europe*, 251.

[188] Franklin Delano Roosevelt, "Wireless to the London Conference," American Presidency Project, University of California, July 3, 1933, http://www.presidency.ucsb.edu/ws/?pid=14679.

The crisis of the economy revived the war debt debates of the 1920s. On December 23, 1931, Hoover had signed a one-year moratorium on war reparations and debts to ease the international economic crisis.[189] As Duroselle writes, France and Britain's refusal to resume payments in late 1932 was not very popular with the U.S. taxpayers and the Congress.[190] Hoover, still in office, leaned toward canceling the debts. In an address to Congress on December 19, 1932, he said, "The discussion of debts is necessarily connected with the solution of major problems at the World Economic Conference. ... Our representatives ... should exchange views upon the debt questions with certain nations at once."[191] The Congress, however, denied Hoover's plans, and, when taking office, FDR did nothing against it, Duroselle writes.[192] To uphold a stable postwar order, it would have been necessary to support the economic recovery of Europe and not to break with the former partners.

Public opinion in the 1930s fully merited the label "isolationist." Herring explains that, with the increasing risk of an East Asian and a European conflict, the United States turned inward and focused on domestic challenges; the public wanted to "retain freedom of action and avoid war at virtually any cost."[193] Peace activism flourished and politicians, veteran groups, and women's organizations formed the backbone of the peace movement. According to Jonas, isolationists came from a wide political and ideological spectrum and formed organizations such as the National Council for the Prevention of War or the Women's International League for Peace and Freedom (WILPF). One also found such individuals as aviator hero Charles a. Lindbergh and

---

[189] Herbert Hoover, "Statement on Signing the Foreign Debt Moratorium Resolution," American Presidency Project, University of California, December 23, 1931, http://www.presidency.ucsb.edu/ws/?pid=22955.

[190] Duroselle, *From Wilson to Roosevelt*, 232–33.

[191] Herbert Hoover, "Special Message to the Congress on Intergovernmental Debts and International Economic Conditions," American Presidency Project, University of California, December 19, 1932, http://www.presidency.ucsb.edu/ws/index.php?pid=23390&st=debts&st1=.

[192] Duroselle, *From Wilson to Roosevelt*, 233.

[193] Herring, *From Colony to Superpower*, 502.

Senator Hiram W. Johnson of California, who fought for U.S. neutrality.[194]

Anne Marie Pois stresses that the pacifist WILPF initially identified itself as internationalist in the Wilsonian sense, but turned to neutralism when confronted with the failure of the League of Nations to solve the conflicts in Europe and Asia, and widely became associated with isolationism.[195] Lindbergh, according to Jonas, enjoyed great popularity, and he asserted that non-involvement would best serve America's interests and thus minimized the German threat.[196]

Activists and interest groups were able to mobilize the masses. For instance, as Herring describes, in April 1935, more than 150,000 students protested on 130 campuses against war, and the number rose to 500,000 in the following year.[197] On April 6, 1937, the 20th anniversary of America's entry into the First World War was celebrated with rallies in more than 2,000 cities and on 500 campuses; 95 percent of Americans did not want the nation to join any future war at the height of the peace movement in 1937.[198] In other words, public resistance against intervention in foreign affairs formed a united front. During President Wilson's second term, FDR—as the nominee for vice-president—had witnessed how fast public opinion could turn against a politician. So, he avoided the minefield of foreign politics as he faced an almost entirely isolationist electorate.

The public's isolationist penchant manifested in political action. In 1934, the Congress passed a bill, named after isolationist Senator Johnson, that prohibited banks from making loans to unwilling war debt

---

[194] Manfred Jonas, *Isolationism in America, 1935–1941* (New York: Cornell University Press, 1966), 32, 42.

[195] Anne Marie Pois, "The U.S. Women's International League for Peace and Freedom and American Neutrality, 1935–1939," *Peace & Change* 14, no. 3 (1989): 267–68.

[196] Jonas, *Isolationism in America*, 98, 249; see also Herring, *From Colony to Superpower*, 521.

[197] Herring, *From Colony to Superpower*, 504.

[198] Ibid.

payers.[199] On January 16, 1935, FDR asked the Senate to agree on the U.S. membership in the World Court since "when every act is of moment to the future of world peace, the United States has an opportunity once more to throw its weight into the scale in favor of peace."[200] According to Herring, however, the Senate rejected the proposal "primarily [because] of continuing hostility to the League of Nations and rising anti-foreignism."[201]

Since the early days of the First World War, as Jonas explains, the WILPF had called for an investigation into the role of the munitions industry in the war, and finally found the support of Republican Senator Gerald P. Nye of North Dakota. On March 12, 1934, Nye introduced Senate Resolution 206, which proposed to set up a special committee—the so-called Nye Committee—for identifying the culprits behind the disaster of the First World War.[202] According to Duroselle, Nye's explanation was simple: America's main motive was the freedom of the seas for trading munitions and raw materials with the belligerent parties, and the bankers had forced the United States into war to ensure the repayment of money that the allies owed to them.[203] As Jonas states, the Nye-Committee proposed a ban on credits for belligerents as well as mandatory neutrality legislation to safeguard the administration from external pressure.[204] Harper points out that even FDR invited Nye to push for legal safeguards to prevent the United States being dragged into war as had happened in 1917.[205]

The plan, however, backfired because the Senate's neutrality legislation was stricter than the president anticipated. Harper writes that FDR

---

[199] "The Johnson Act: Extension of Credit to a Government in Default." *Columbia Law Review* 35, no. 1 (1935): 102. doi:10.2307/1116369.

[200] Franklin Delano Roosevelt, "Message to the Senate in re World Court," FDR Library's Digital Collections, University of Illinois, January 16, 1935, http://www.fdrlibrary.marist.edu/_resources/images/msf/msf00781.

[201] Herring, *From Colony to Superpower*, 504.

[202] Jonas, *Isolationism in America*, 142–43.

[203] Duroselle, *From Wilson to Roosevelt*, 238–39.

[204] Jonas, *Isolationism in America*, 146.

[205] Harper, *American Visions of Europe*, 66.

initially wanted the freedom of discretion to apply sanctions on belligerent parties selectively.[206] As Duroselle asserts, faced with the war between Italy and Ethiopia, the Senate imposed an automatic embargo on arms and loans on all belligerents once they were in the state of war to deprive the president of any possibility of distinguishing between aggressors and victims.[207] Since FDR needed the support of the Congress for crucial domestic legislation, he signed the neutrality law on August 31, 1935, Herring explains.[208] Disappointed, the president commented on his decision: "It is the policy of this Government to avoid being drawn into wars between other Nations, but it is a fact that no Congress and no Executive can foresee all possible future situations."[209] In other words, instead of receiving a guidance that would provide the president some freedom of action, FDR now confronted a strict neutrality law that immobilized his agency in foreign politics.

The Italo-Ethiopian War revealed problems of diverging public interests and neutrality legislation. When the war between Italy and Ethiopia broke out on October 3, 1935, according to Jonas, FDR struggled to implement neutrality laws because such measures would affect the Ethiopian side more.[210] Finally, however, the president implemented an arms embargo in accordance with the Neutrality Act, restricted travel on belligerents' vessels, and prohibited making loans to Italy in accordance with the Johnson Act.[211] As Herring explains, Ethiopia was of great importance for African Americans, and for the first time African Americans involved themselves in the foreign policy debate, protested against Italian aggression, and even boycotted Italian-American businesses.[212]

---

[206] Harper, *American Visions of Europe*, 66.

[207] Duroselle, *From Wilson to Roosevelt*, 240.

[208] Herring, *From Colony to Superpower*, 505.

[209] Franklin Delano Roosevelt, "Statement on Neutrality Legislation," American Presidency Project, University of California, August 31, 1935, http://www.presidency.ucsb.edu/ws/index.php?pid=14927.

[210] Jonas, *Isolationism in America*, 172.

[211] United States Department of State, *Peace and War: United States Foreign Policy, 1931–1941* (Washington, DC: GPO, 1943), 31.

[212] Herring, *From Colony to Superpower*, 506.

According to Duroselle, the League of Nations declared Italy the aggressor and imposed sanctions showing only minor effect because the United States still supplied Mussolini with large quantities of raw materials such as oil and copper.[213] Hull criticized the amorality of such sales and announced on November 15, 1935, "This class of trade is directly contrary to the policy of this Government ... as it is also contrary to the general spirit of the recent Neutrality Act."[214] Herring points out the administration's dilemma, because, when the government extended the embargo to strategic supplies and thus shifted to the Ethiopian side, now the Italian-Americans protested.[215]

Furthermore, the embargo caused a slight dent in export rates, Duroselle writes, which alarmed the Congress. This outcome also fostered a mitigation of the first neutrality law, which gave the president leeway to decide whether a state of war existed or not—the Second Neutrality Act of February 29, 1936.[216] In other worlds, diverging public opinion and economic interests diluted strict neutrality and influenced the course of policy.

The Spanish Civil War (1936–1939) posed a new problem for U.S. neutrality. When the conflict broke out in July 1936, the government's policy followed the line of promotion of peace and strict noninterference in foreign conflicts. Yet, the legal status of the Spanish conflict caused a problem. In a telegram to the diplomatic and consular officers in the United States and Spain on August 7, 1936, Hull clarified, "It is clear that our Neutrality Law ... has no application in the present situation, since that applies only in the event of war between or among nations. ... This Government will, of course, scrupulously refrain from any interference whatsoever in the unfortunate Spanish situation."[217] In a speech at Chautauqua, New York, on August 14, 1936, FDR announced that the United States was not isolationist per se, but it would

---

[213] Duroselle, *From Wilson to Roosevelt*, 241.
[214] United States Department of State, *Peace and War*, 293.
[215] Herring, *From Colony to Superpower*, 507.
[216] Duroselle, *From Wilson to Roosevelt*, 241–42; United States Department of State, *Peace and War*, 313.
[217] United States Department of State, *Peace and War*, 322–23.

like to isolate itself generally from all wars; however, as long as war exists there would be the danger of being drawn into it.[218] Ultimately, FDR understood that America might not be able to sustain strict neutrality.

Despite initial doubts, the United States imposed the neutrality law on the conflict in Spain. After months of inactivity in the course of the 1936 election campaign, on January 8, 1937, Congress almost unanimously passed a special bill that put an arms embargo on both sides of the Spanish Civil War, Duroselle reports.[219] This decision, however, caused a bitter U.S. domestic controversy. Political scientist Dominic Tierney explains that the Spanish Nationalists under General Francisco Franco received military assistance from Germany and Italy, whereas the U.S. embargo strongly impaired the left-leaning Spanish Republic.[220] In response, U.S. liberals, socialists, and communists campaigned for lifting the sanctions against Spain. On the other hand, Roman Catholic interest groups saw the war as a conflict between Christianity and communism and thus insisted on the embargo; unfortunately, both factions were the pillars of FDR's New Deal coalition.[221] Once again, public interests put pressure on political decision-making.

Finally, Roosevelt and Congress agreed on a strict neutrality policy, but the Congress wanted to go even further and make the neutrality laws permanent, Duroselle asserts.[222] As a result, on May 1, 1937, the president signed the Third Neutrality Act, which was unlimited, and continued the embargo provisions of the previous law. The law, however, now had two additional clauses: first, it forbade U.S. citizens to travel on belligerent ships; second, it included goods other than war material for which "cash and carry" regulations were introduced, which

---

[218] United States Department of State, *Peace and War*, 325–26.

[219] Duroselle, *From Wilson to Roosevelt*, 242–43.

[220] Dominic Tierney, *FDR and the Spanish Civil War: Neutrality and Commitment in the Struggle that Divided America* (London: Duke, 2007), 4, 5.

[221] Ibid., 4, 5.

[222] Duroselle, *From Wilson to Roosevelt*, 244.

allowed receiving commodities only in exchange for immediate payment.[223] Neutrality was now at its height.

4. July 1937 to June 1940—The End of Neutrality

A new war in North East Asia put neutrality to the test. In July 1937, just two months after the signing of the Third Neutrality Act, the Sino-Japanese War broke out. The fighting was characterized by heavy losses on the Chinese side and harsh brutality by the Japanese, Herring writes.[224] The conflict divided the U.S. public since, in the eyes of many, the Japanese were still a bulwark against Soviet Russia, and trade with Japan flourished; on the other hand, people sympathized with the Chinese, especially after reports that Japanese soldiers raped countless women after taking the city of Nanking.[225] The United States struggled about the best political course.

The answer reflected the public's ambivalence. Jonas writes that most isolationists insisted on invoking neutrality legislation, but the president refused to declare the state of war between China and Japan since an embargo would only benefit the Japanese.[226] On September 14, 1937, FDR prohibited the use of government-owned merchant vessels to transport implements of war, and all other ships acted at own risk; on the other hand, "The question of applying the Neutrality Act remains *in status quo*," he said.[227] Unsurprisingly, the president's political course did not remain unnoticed. In July 1937, the pro-Roosevelt political scientist Charles Austin Beard wrote that "the American people may well prepare themselves to see President Roosevelt plunge the country into the European War, when it comes, far more quickly than did President Wilson."[228] In other words, FDR guided the Americans

---

[223] Duroselle, *From Wilson to Roosevelt*, 244.

[224] Herring, *From Colony to Superpower*, 511.

[225] Ibid.

[226] Jonas, *Isolationism in America*, 200–1.

[227] United States Department of State, *Peace and War*, 380.

[228] Quoted in Charles Austin Beard, *American Foreign Policy in the Making, 1932–1940: A Study in Responsibilities* (New Haven: Yale University Press, 1946), 182.

toward a less neutral foreign policy, which included an inherent risk of being plunged into a future war.

The display of this new policy was FDR's famous Quarantine Speech, which marked the beginning of abandoning neutrality and advocating the importance of democratic values. In 1937, despite the beginning of a new recession (1937–1938), the president's concern shifted toward foreign policy because the crises in the Far East and Europe had shown the inadequacy of neutrality; furthermore, as Duroselle writes, FDR had recognized that isolationism was not a realistic option for the United States, though he was still in favor of neutrality.[229] Jonas asserts that, in earlier conflicts, U.S. neutrality had willingly or unwillingly supported either one or the other side, and the attempt to force the administration into inactiveness by law had not eliminated the country's importance as a player in foreign conflicts.[230] In other words, it was impossible for isolationists to find a policy course that did not affect foreign wars. Meanwhile, American neutrality created a situation in which other nations dictated war and peace in the world, Jonas writes.[231] The Quarantine Speech on October 5, 1937, revealed that the president was willing to change this situation. He said:

> The peace-loving nations must make a concerted effort in opposition to those violations of treaties and those ignorings of humane instincts which today are creating a state of international anarchy and instability from which there is no escape through mere isolation or neutrality. ... There is a solidarity and interdependence about the modern world, both technically and morally, which makes it impossible for any nation completely to isolate itself from economic and political upheavals in the rest of the world. ... It is, therefore, a matter of vital interest and concern to the people of the United States that the sanctity of international treaties and the maintenance of international morality be restored. ... It

---

[229] Duroselle, *From Wilson to Roosevelt*, 246–47.
[230] Jonas, *Isolationism in America*, 203.
[231] Ibid., 204.

> seems to be unfortunately true that the epidemic of world lawlessness is spreading. When an epidemic of physical disease starts to spread, the community approves and joins in a quarantine of the patients in order to protect the health of the community against the spread of the disease. It is my determination to pursue a policy of peace. It is my determination to adopt every practicable measure to avoid involvement in war. ... America hates war. America hopes for peace. Therefore, America actively engages in the search for peace.[232]

FDR made it clear that the country could not isolate itself from the rest of the world. The maintenance of international norms and morality became a vital interest of the American people and needed a concerted effort. To pursue this approach, one must clearly distinguish between the healthy nations and those aggressors who had to be quarantined.

The American public in 1937, however, was not ready to accept FDR's new internationalist policy. Unfortunately, as Duroselle writes, the president had drafted the Quarantine Speech without the help of Hull, and the Secretary of State now confronted a massive wave of isolationist protest while the Congress was just at the height of isolationist sentiment.[233] Unabashed, FDR believed that an education process would persuade his people of a necessary foreign policy change.[234]

The sinking of the U.S. river gunboat *Panay* by Japanese aircraft on December 12, 1937, fostered a new attack on the president's agency. Jonas writes that Senator Louis Leon Ludlow of Indiana sponsored a constitutional amendment that would require a public referendum prior to any declaration of war; now, the *Panay* incident gave Ludlow the necessary support to bring the proposal to the floor. The amendment received widespread support from isolationists and pressure

---

[232] Franklin Delano Roosevelt, "Quarantine Speech," Miller Center, University of Virginia, October 5, 1937, http://millercenter.org/president/speeches/speech-3310.

[233] Duroselle, *From Wilson to Roosevelt*, 250.

[234] Ibid.

groups such as the WILPF, but the proposal was narrowly defeated.[235] Facing such a constitutional hurdle, the United States would almost never be able to enter a war. However, the country remained resolutely isolationist.

FDR undertook a last attempt to preserve peace. In October 1937, according to William Leonard Langer and Sarell Everett Gleason, the president planned to invite all diplomatic representatives in Washington on Armistice Day (November 11) of the following year to his presentation of a proposal for a new peace agreement. This agreement should focus on basic principles of international relations, the freedom of access to raw materials, methods for pacifically revising international agreements, the laws and customs of warfare on land and sea, and the rights of neutrals.[236] Nevertheless, with Italy, Germany, and Japan "arming to the teeth," as Duroselle concludes, such an effort was "extremely naïve," and it finally failed because the British rejected the plans in January 1938.[237]

Convinced by the British refusal to accept that the United States alone would not be able to ensure peace, FDR turned his attention toward the strengthening of the national defense. In a message to Congress on January 28, 1938, he said, "As Commander-in-Chief ... it is my constitutional duty to report to the Congress that our national defense is, in the light of the increasing armaments of other nations, inadequate for purposes of national security and requires increase for that reason."[238] The United States needed to prepare for a possible war.

Surprisingly, even isolationists substantially supported America's military preparedness. Jonas asserts that some isolationists recognized the strengthening of the military as a step toward war, but even those who believed in America's favorable geographical position were not

---

[235] Jonas, *Isolationism in America*, 162–63.

[236] William Leonard Langer and Sarell Everett Gleason, *The Challenge to Isolation, 1937–1940* (New York: Harper, 1952), 22.

[237] Duroselle, *From Wilson to Roosevelt*, 250–51.

[238] United States Department of State, *Peace and War*, 403–4.

unaware of the effects of a powerful Navy and Army.[239] Without substantial opposition and although isolationists controlled the Congress until 1939, the Congress granted more than $17 billion for national defense in the last few years before America's entry into the war, and isolationists even showed the willingness to expand the U.S. military establishment to provide an impregnable defense.[240]

Besides increasing the country's preparedness, the events in Europe accelerated the revision of U.S. foreign policy. Duroselle points out that Austria's *Anschluss* with Germany in March 1938 caused almost no reaction among the U.S. public.[241] During the Czech crisis in summer 1938, Hitler ironically used the "Wilsonian banner of self-determination" to justify his policy, first demanding autonomy for the German speaking population of the Sudeten region in Czechoslovakia, and later calling for the secession of the entire Sudeten territory, Herring asserts.[242] Tensions between Czechoslovakia and Germany reached a climax in late summer 1938, and it became clear that Hitler insisted on his claims even at the risk of war, which encouraged Britain and France to take the initiative to solve the crisis.[243] On September 26, 1938, FDR sent a personal message to the heads of the governments of Czechoslovakia, France, Germany, and Great Britain, stating,

> The supreme desire of the American people is to live in peace. ... Every civilized nation of the world voluntarily assumed the solemn obligations of the Kellogg-Briand Pact of 1928 to solve controversies only by pacific methods. ... On behalf of the 130 millions of people of the United States of America and for the sake of humanity everywhere I most earnestly appeal to you not to break off negotiations looking to a peaceful, fair, and constructive settlement of the questions at issue.[244]

---

[239] Jonas, *Isolationism in America*, 129.
[240] Ibid., 132–33.
[241] Duroselle, *From Wilson to Roosevelt*, 255.
[242] Herring, *From Colony to Superpower*, 513.
[243] Ibid.
[244] United States Department of State, *Peace and War*, 425.

FDR still believed in a peaceful solution of the crisis. His message, however, made it clear that the United States wanted no political entanglements in Europe. The Europeans should solve their problems on their own. Finally, as Herring explains, on September 29, 1938, at a conference in Munich, the parties agreed to turn over the Sudeten territory to Germany in exchange for a guarantee of Czechoslovakia's new borders.[245] At first glance, the results of the Munich conference confirmed the U.S. course. Munich, however, became a synonym for an unsuccessful appeasement policy and the folly of negotiating with aggressors. Herring points out that for Hitler Munich was a defeat because he wanted war whereas the other nations were not willing to fight.[246]

Apparently, it became clear that even the Western powers would not be able to stop German expansionism without American help. According to historian David Reynolds, FDR was convinced that Germany's air superiority had changed the world's balance of power, and therefore he sought congressional support for a massive increase in aircraft production and even tried to repeal the arms embargo to support France and Britain.[247] At a military conference on November 14, 1938, as Duroselle reports, FDR announced that the United States must increase the production of airplanes to a rate of 24,000 per year—twice the number Germany was able to produce.[248] In other words, the president had plans for an unneutral rearmament of the European democracies by every possible means. Such a plan would need congressional support.

The Congress, however, opposed any changes to existing neutrality laws. According to the law, an arms supply for France and Britain would come to a halt as soon as war broke out. Hence, on May 27, 1939, Hull urged for an adaptation of the arms embargo in a letter to Congress. He wrote, "What we should try to do for the purpose of

---

[245] Herring, *From Colony to Superpower*, 513.

[246] Ibid., 514.

[247] David Reynolds, *From Munich to Pearl Harbor: Roosevelt's America and the Origins of the Second World War* (Chicago: Ivan R. Dee, 2001), 45–46.

[248] Duroselle, *From Wilson to Roosevelt*, 256.

keeping this country out of war is to enact measures adapted to the safeguarding of our interests. ... It does not require that a neutral nation shall embargo any articles destined for belligerents."[249] The Congress remained unimpressed, and on July 11, 1939, the Senate decided to defer action on neutrality legislation until the next session of Congress.[250] It would take more to break the resistance of Congress.

The war came in September 1939. Germany invaded Czechia in March 1939, which encouraged the British and French to extend their military commitments to Poland. On August 23, 1939, Hitler secured his eastern flank by negotiating a non-aggression pact with Russia, dividing Eastern Europe into spheres of influence, and on September 1, 1939, Germany invaded Poland. In return, the Western allies declared war on Germany. In a radio message on September 3, 1939, FDR addressed the American people

> I had hoped ... that some miracle would prevent a devastating war in Europe ... This will be followed by a Proclamation required by the existing Neutrality Act. ... This nation will remain a neutral nation, but I cannot ask that every American remain neutral in thought as well. ... I hope the United States will keep out of this war."[251]

In other words, the United States wanted to prevent any entanglement in the European conflict but actually felt a moral obligation to act.

As FDR had promised, he grudgingly invoked neutrality law on September 5, 1939, henceforth denying war materials to the belligerents, Herring writes.[252] In contrast to 1914, Duroselle points out, the public opinion was unanimous against Germany, and even the German-

---

[249] United States Department of State, *Peace and War*, 462.

[250] Ibid., 66.

[251] Franklin Delano Roosevelt, "Fireside Chat," American Presidency Project, University of California, September 3, 1939, http://www.presidency.ucsb.edu/ws/?pid=15801.

[252] Herring, *From Colony to Superpower*, 517.

Americans were against Hitler's policy. Nonetheless, the public still opposed an active participation in war.[253] As a result of the invocation of neutrality, some war material, waiting for shipment to France and Britain, had already been immobilized in port.[254] To further aid European democracies, FDR had to circumvent existing neutrality legislation. So, in an address to Congress on November 21, 1939, he recommended repealing the arms embargo and keeping U.S. citizens and ships out of dangerous areas to prevent conflicts that might involve the country in war.[255] Although some hardline isolationists still opposed changes to the neutrality law, the majority of Congress was now willing to pass a new Neutrality Act.[256] Reynolds writes that the new law substituted the arms embargo by a cash and carry clause, in which the buyer was responsible for the transport of the goods; since France and England had naval superiority, the new law was clearly discriminatory—a well-known issue that conformed to the president's and public's opinion.[257] De facto, by supporting the Western powers, the United States now became a co-belligerent.

The period of inaction in fall and winter 1939 and 1940—the Phony War—ended abruptly with Hitler's blitzkrieg warfare against Scandinavia, the Low Countries, and France. Hitler completed in less than three months what Kaiser Wilhelm II did not accomplish in four years. Furthermore, Britain suffered significant losses of war material in Dunkirk and was now alone against Germany. According to Herring, the fall of France caught the Americans by surprise, and for the first time they felt vulnerable to events abroad.[258] In his address to Congress on January 3, 1940, FDR warned that

> American citizens will ... feel the shock of events on other continents. ... The overwhelming majority of our fellow citizens do not abandon in the slightest their

---

[253] Duroselle, *From Wilson to Roosevelt*, 260.
[254] Ibid.
[255] United States Department of State, *Peace and War*, 487.
[256] Duroselle, *From Wilson to Roosevelt*, 260.
[257] Reynolds, *From Munich to Pearl Harbor*, 65–67.
[258] Herring, *From Colony to Superpower*, 519–20.

hope and expectation that the United States will not become involved in military participation in the war. ... But there is a vast difference between keeping out of war and pretending that this war is none of our business. ... The future world will be a shabby and dangerous place to live in—even for Americans.[259]

The nation had too long taken its security for granted and shielded itself against the bitter reality. European instability directly affected U.S. security.

5. June 1940 to December 1941—America's Entry into the War

The defeat of France in summer 1940 triggered the end of anti-war sentiments. Since FDR was obsessed with maximizing public support, it had become common practice, as Herring points out, that the White House monitored subversive groups, even by illegal means, and gathered information about anti-interventionists' activities to gain advantages in policy debates.[260] With the pressing events in Europe, the year 1940 saw a significant rupture in anti-war sentiments. In May 1940, as Duroselle explains, 64 percent of Americans believed that their country should stay out of war, but after Hitler's stunning victory over France this number dropped to 37 percent in December.[261] In June 1940, 86 percent of the people were against war, but that number dropped to 69 percent in September 1941, and 61 percent wanted to aid Britain even though it involved a serious risk of war.[262] As a result, in October 1941, 85 percent of Americans believed that the country would go to war.[263] Interestingly, the support for a war against Germany was stronger among supporters of the Democratic Party than among Republicans, with a significantly lower level of support in the

---

[259] United States Department of State, *Peace and War*, 508.
[260] Herring, *From Colony to Superpower*, 520, 537.
[261] Duroselle, *From Wilson to Roosevelt*, 272.
[262] Ibid., 272, 273.
[263] Ibid., 272.

Midwest.[264] Nevertheless, the defeat of France figured prominently in the gradually increasing support for an active involvement in the European conflict.

In November 1941, shortly before the Japanese attack on Pearl Harbor, 47 percent of the Americans were in favor of sending a large army to Europe to defeat Germany; 46 percent were against an intervention.[265] In other words, for the first time, a majority of the populace supported an active involvement in the European war. The attack on Pearl Harbor on December 7, 1941, then broke all dams, and 96 percent of the people approved the declaration of war against Japan.[266] In sum, the defeat of France fostered the insight that non-involvement was not a realistic option, and, by the end of 1941, the public was convinced that the United States must enter the war.

Pressure groups played a vital role in shaping public opinion. From 1940 to 1941, pressure groups had strong ties with the U.S. government. For instance, as historian Melvin Small explains, FDR encouraged William Allen White to form the Committee to Defend America by Aiding the Allies (CDA) to mobilize public support and educate the people about the fascist threat.[267] The CDA, according to Duroselle, had 750 chapters and 10,000 active members, and it organized lectures, published articles, and lobbied in Washington for increasing the aid to Britain.[268]

The public, however, was unaware of the ties between the CDA and the government and the questionable methods these entities used to influence the people. For example, as historian Wayne S. Cole explains, the Roosevelt administration supported the CDA with inside infor-

---

[264] Duroselle, *From Wilson to Roosevelt*, 273.
[265] Ibid., 274.
[266] Ibid.
[267] Melvin Small, *Democracy & Diplomacy: The Impact of Domestic Politics on U.S. Foreign Policy 1789–1994* (Baltimore: John Hopkins University Press, 1996), 70.
[268] Duroselle, *From Wilson to Roosevelt*, 275.

mation, and the committee became the "unofficial public relations organization for President Roosevelt's foreign office."[269] Duroselle asserts that the CDA wanted to increase any help for Britain, short of war, to keep the United States out of the conflict, but a splinter movement within the CDA, the Fight for Freedom Committee, favored U.S. involvement in the war and later became the major pro-war pressure group.[270]

The opposition also had pressure groups of which the America First Committee was the most ambitious. Cole explains that the Committee was founded on September 19, 1940, and by December 1941, it had about 850,000 members; among them were manufacturers and bankers, influential Republican politicians, Catholic bishops and priests, and labor leaders.[271] The America First Committee, as Cole further writes, unsuccessfully opposed nearly all war-related measures of the administration in the following months, such as the Lend-Lease Act, convoys, FDR's "shoot-on-sight policy," or the repeal of provisions of the Neutrality Act; the Committee was convinced "that America could not solve Europe's problems nor police the world."[272] Since the government actively pushed the public toward a more interventionist foreign policy with the help of the CDA, it was hard for the isolationist opposition to stand its ground.

The presidential election campaign in 1940 did not bring an isolationist debate to the forefront. FDR had decided to break with the two-term tradition and the Democrats nominated him on the first ballot. According to Duroselle, the Republicans did not want to go into harsh opposition and refused to support the isolationist candidate Thomas E. Dewey; instead, the delegates voted for the dark horse candidate, internationalist Wendell Willkie, who supported the CDA's position to increase help to Britain.[273] Historian Justus D. Doenecke writes that,

---

[269] Wayne S. Cole, *America First: The Battle against Intervention, 1940-1941* (New York: Octagon Books, 1971), 7.

[270] Duroselle, *From Wilson to Roosevelt*, 275–76.

[271] Cole, *America First*, 19, 21–22, 30.

[272] Ibid., 37, 56.

[273] Duroselle, *From Wilson to Roosevelt*, 277–78.

although both candidates' positions on foreign policy were similar, Willkie's campaign focused on the people's fear of being dragged into the European war.[274]

On September 16, 1940, FDR established the first peacetime draft in U.S. history, the Selective Training and Service Act, which affected more than 800,000 men.[275] During the election campaign, such a step, of course, played into Willkie's hands, but FDR countered and promised at a campaign address in Boston on October 30, 1940, that he would not send American soldiers into foreign wars, instead they should "keep the threat of war far away from our shores. The purpose of our defense is defense."[276]

The transcript of the speech that was later distributed omits an important detail. Reynolds writes that in the actual address, FDR had made the exception that his promise was not valid in the case of a foreign attack: "That is going to beat me!" Willkie said.[277] So it happened, and FDR gained a clear-cut victory in the election a week thereafter. Since the large number of isolationists did not have a spokesman for their interests, they voted for Willkie more out of hate for FDR than out of true support for Willkie, Duroselle writes.[278] The president's policy was now lacking a true anti-war opposition, and he could carry on with his interventionist policy.

American foreign policy needed backing by a military strategy. On November 4, 1940, one day before the election, the U.S. military presented Plan Dog. According to Trachtenberg, Plan Dog anticipated a principal war effort directed toward Germany, with only limited operations against Japan.[279] As Stetson Conn and Byron Fairchild write, the

---

[274] Justus D. Doenecke, *Storm on the Horizon: The Challenge to American Intervention, 1939–1941* (New York: Rowman & Littlefield, 2003), 161.

[275] United States Department of State, *Peace and War*, 84.

[276] Franklin D. Roosevelt, "Campaign Address at Boston," The American Presidency Project, University of California, October 30, 1940, http://www.presidency.ucsb.edu/ws/?pid=15887.

[277] Reynolds, *From Munich to Pearl Harbor*, 101.

[278] Duroselle, *From Wilson to Roosevelt*, 278.

[279] Trachtenberg, *Craft of International History*, 118.

plan included a major offensive across the Atlantic with initially naval forces but probably also a large ground operation from Africa or Western Europe, meanwhile maintaining the defensive in the Pacific.[280] This Europe-first strategy was in line with FDR's ideas that the United States could no longer think in purely continental terms. Britain's collapse and a Europe under German control threatened the Western hemisphere. Trachtenberg explains that the planners were convinced that the United States had to intervene quickly before Germany controlled the continent and had full access to the resources of the conquered territory; the British fleet played a vital role in checking Germany's superpower.[281] In late 1940, however, it was not yet the time to pursue such a strategy openly.

The most important problem now was to help Britain, which stood alone against the Axis powers. According to Reynolds, on May 15 and on July 30, 1940, British Prime Minister Winston Churchill appealed for military equipment, especially destroyers, but FDR deflected the requests since such a deal would need congressional approval, which was unlikely because of a new law from July 2, 1940, prohibiting the trade of surplus equipment that was essential for U.S. defense.[282] Alarmed by considerations about the role of the British fleet in limiting Germany's power in the Atlantic—later expressed in Plan Dog—the president decided to circumvent the law. As Herring explains, FDR urged top military leaders to declare ships obsolete for national defense and encouraged the CDA to stimulate a public debate.[283] In return, as Doenecke asserts, Churchill agreed on a 99-year lease for the construction of naval bases on eight British territories.[284] Herring reveals that the president, through the CDA, also ensured that his republican opponent Willkie would not interfere with the deal or make it an issue

---

[280] Stetson Conn, Byron Fairchild, and Center of Military History, *The Framework of Hemisphere Defense* (Washington, DC: Center of Military History, U.S. Army, 1989), 91.

[281] Trachtenberg, *Craft of International History*, 118–19.

[282] Reynolds, *From Munich to Pearl Harbor*, 82, 83–84.

[283] Herring, *From Colony to Superpower*, 522.

[284] Doenecke, *Storm on the Horizon*, 125.

during the election campaign.²⁸⁵ FDR had prepared the field for his next move.

On September 3, 1940, FDR notified the Congress that the U.S. government had acquired the right to lease naval and air bases "in exchange for fifty of our over-age destroyers."²⁸⁶ Although the deal was a deliberate break of U.S. neutrality legislation, the American people welcomed the aid to Britain, as Doenecke confirms.²⁸⁷ The president avoided a congressional say in the destroyer-bases deal by using an executive order, referring to a 1936 Supreme Court decision that confirmed that the federal government did not need congressional authority to act in foreign affairs. Herring concludes that this act was FDR's "boldest—and most questionable—move" stretching his "constitutional authority beyond generally acknowledged bonds."²⁸⁸ Actively equipping Britain with war material, the president tied the country closer to Britain and made a great step toward a U.S. involvement in war, but he also provoked an open conflict with the Congress.

Supporting Britain against German aggression became a moral obligation. Duroselle explains that, after the clear-cut reelection, the president—surprisingly—did not seem to be willing to immediately strengthen the country's war effort and increase aid to Britain; instead, he conducted a post-campaign cruise aboard the U.S. cruiser *Tuscaloosa*.²⁸⁹ On December 8, 1940, as Doenecke reports, FDR received a letter from Churchill asking for a revision of the neutrality laws since Britain was no longer able to pay for war supplies; cash and carry was no longer an option.²⁹⁰ The president recognized the urgency in the British plea and, in a press conference on December 17, 1940, he explained that "the best defense of Great Britain is the best defense of the United States. ... Now, what I am trying to do is to ... get rid of the

---

285 Herring, *From Colony to Superpower*, 522.
286 United States Department of State, *Peace and War*, 565.
287 Doenecke, *Storm on the Horizon*, 125.
288 Herring, *From Colony to Superpower*, 523.
289 Duroselle, *From Wilson to Roosevelt*, 287.
290 Doenecke, *Storm on the Horizon*, 166.

silly, foolish old dollar sign."[291] In other words, FDR was planning a new attack on the neutrality legislation.

In a speech on December 29, 1940, FDR prepared the battlefield: "We must be the great arsenal of democracy. For us this is an emergency as serious as war itself," he said.[292] In his annual message to Congress on January 6, 1940, he further emphasized, "In the future days, which we seek to make secure, we look forward to a world founded upon four essential human freedoms, ... freedom of speech and expression, ... freedom of every person to worship God, ... freedom from want, ... [and] freedom from fear ... anywhere in the world."[293] These announcements gave the debate a moral tone. It was now a moral obligation for the United States to help Britain and secure freedom in the world.

With his renewed call to Congress, the president was playing a dangerous political game. FDR's executive order on the destroyer-bases deal had stretched the relationship with Congress to the limit. Now the president needed to reassure congressional support for obtaining unprecedented authority to lend war material to any nation whose defense he thought to be essential for the security of the United States.[294] On October 9, 1941, FDR explained to Congress, "The Neutrality Act of 1939 was passed at a time when the true magnitude of the Nazi attempt to dominate the world was visualized by few persons. ... We Americans have never been neutral in thought. ... The Neutrality Act requires a

---

[291] Franklin D. Roosevelt: "Press Conference," American Presidency Project, University of California, December 17, 1940, http://www.presidency.ucsb.edu/ws/?pid=15913.

[292] Franklin D. Roosevelt, "Fireside Chat.," American Presidency Project, University of California, December 29, 1940, http://www.presidency.ucsb.edu/ws/?pid=15917.

[293] Franklin D. Roosevelt, "President Franklin Roosevelt's Annual Message to Congress" 100 Milestone Documents, U.S. National Archives and Records Administration, January 9, 1941, https://www.ourdocuments.gov/doc.php?doc=70&page=transcript.

[294] Herring, *From Colony to Superpower*, 525.

complete reconsideration in the light of known facts."[295] The bill, designated HR 1776 and entitled "An Act to Further Promote the Defense of the United States, and for Other Purposes," authorized FDR to trade war materials to "any country whose defense the President deems vital to the defense of the United States."[296] The other side of the coin was that now the United States would have to ensure the safe delivery of goods, which most likely would lead to military involvement.

Although the risk of war was obvious, Congress approved the president's proposal. According to Herring, FDR knew that the bill had a solid backing from the public and from both houses, and he even had support from his former adversary Willkie, who warned that the Lend-Lease Act was the only chance to defend the country's liberty without going to war on its own.[297] Cole writes that the America First Committee referred to the Land-Lease Act as the "War Bill," and the committee released a massive campaign against the act.[298] Critics argued that trade with Britain would require convoys that could provoke a German attack and could drag the country into war. For instance, the America First Committee released a declaration that warned, "In 1917 we sent our American ships into the war zone and this led us to war. In 1941 we must keep our naval convoys and merchant vessels on this side of the Atlantic."[299] Senator Burton Kendall Wheeler asserted that the Lend-Lease program "would plow under every fourth American boy."[300] Isolationists' arguments, however, fell on deaf ears. The Congress passed the bill with partisan majorities and the president signed it on March 11, 1941. The Lend-Lease Act violated the cash-and-carry rule of the Neutrality Laws as well as the lending restrictions of the

---

[295] United States Department of State, *Peace and War*, 761–65.

[296] "Land Lease Bill," 100 Milestone Documents, U.S. National Archives and Records Administration, March 11, 1941, https://www.ourdocuments.gov/doc.php?doc=71&page=transcript.

[297] Herring, *From Colony to Superpower*, 525.

[298] Cole, *America First*, 46.

[299] Quoted in Ibid., 156.

[300] Quoted in Robert Dallek, *Franklin D. Roosevelt and American Foreign Policy, 1932–1945* (New York: Oxford University Press, 1979), 259.

Johnson Act. Finally, the United States was on the same road that had led the country to war in 1917.

The unimpeded trade with Britain raised the question of the security of the convoys. Historian Robert Dallek explains that in spring 1941—as the isolationist opposition had warned—the security of convoys became a major issue because British losses in the Atlantic reached tremendous proportions; consequently, the president gave his initial approval for Navy plans for the protection of the convoys on April 3, 1941.[301] According to Conn and Fairchild, Navy Defense of the Hemisphere Plan Numbers 1 and 2 shifted ships from the Pacific fleet to the Atlantic and extended the U.S. defense perimeter to 25 degrees west longitude (later 26 degrees); American vessels and planes patrolled the area to warn convoys of German submarines, and U.S. ships would attack aggressors after giving warning within a radius of 25 miles around U.S. and British bases.[302] On April 9, 1941, as Duroselle explains, the United States made an agreement with Denmark to place Greenland under temporary protection; Iceland followed in July 1941, and on July 11 Defense of the Hemisphere Number 4 permitted escorting convoys between the U.S. mainland and Iceland.[303]

In sharp contrast to traditional concepts of U.S. defense, the expansion of the defense perimeter far into the western Atlantic showed that the United States now focused on far more than just its mainland. In a radio address on May 27, 1941, the president explained, "When your enemy comes at you in a tank or a bombing plane, if you hold your fire until you see the whites of his eyes, you will never know what hit you. ... Old-fashioned common sense calls for the use of a strategy that will prevent such an enemy from gaining a foothold in the first place."[304]

---

[301] Dallek, *Franklin D. Roosevelt and American Foreign Policy*, 260.

[302] Conn, Fairchild, and Center of Military History, *Framework of Hemisphere Defense*, 105–6.

[303] Duroselle, *From Wilson to Roosevelt*, 295-96.

[304] Franklin Delano Roosevelt, "Radio Address Announcing an Unlimited National Emergency," The American Presidency Project, University of California, May 27, 1941, http://www.presidency.ucsb.edu/ws/?pid=16120.

Hence, FDR formulated an early doctrine of preemption and the conditions for an open conflict were set. It just needed a spark to detonate the powder keg in the North Atlantic.

By September 1941, the United States was in an undeclared naval war with Germany. Herring asserts that Germany's successful attack on the Soviet Union in June 1941 raised U.S. fear of German dominance in Europe, which drew Britain and the United States even closer together and finally pushed FDR toward an active involvement in the Atlantic battle.[305] As though by chance, on September 4, 1941, a German U-boat attacked the destroyer *USS Greer* on its way to Iceland. Dallek writes that the Americans had reported the U-boat's position to a British aircraft, which then engaged the Germans; the U-boat retaliated by firing torpedoes at the *Greer* but missed the ship.[306] On September 11, 1941, concealing the extent to which the United States had provoked the attack, FDR explained that "[for] generation after generation, America has battled for the general policy of the freedom of the seas. ... No Nation has the right to make the broad oceans of the world at great distances from the actual theater of land war unsafe for the commerce of others."[307] Once again, the U.S. focus was on trade issues—a remarkable parallel to Wilson's arguments at the dawn of the First World War.

To demonstrate his decisiveness, in a radio speech on September 11, 1941, FDR announced that American naval vessels and American planes would strike first and would now protect merchant ships under any flag.[308] According to Conn and Fairchild, these plans went into effect as Defense of the Hemisphere Plan Number 5 on September 28, 1941.[309] The president, however, clearly used the *USS Greer* incident to manipulate public opinion in his favor. Cole writes that the America

---

[305] Herring, *From Colony to Superpower*, 533.

[306] Dallek, *Franklin D. Roosevelt and American Foreign Policy*, 287.

[307] Franklin Delano Roosevelt, "Fireside Chat," American Presidency Project University of California, September 11, 1941, http://www.presidency.ucsb.edu/ws/?pid=16012.

[308] Roosevelt, "Fireside Chat," September 11, 1941.

[309] Conn, Fairchild, and Center of Military History, *Framework of Hemisphere Defense*, 134.

First Committee confronted FDR's "shoot-on-sight" policy with a storm of protest, accusing him of trying "to arouse hysteria and plunge us into a foreign war, unwanted by the people."[310] In October, as Dallek reports, attacks on the destroyers *USS Kearny* and *Reuben James* resulted in heavy losses and made it obvious that Germany had modified its policy of not seeking open conflict with the United States.[311] In other words, America was now in an undeclared war with Germany.

Consequently, the United States officially abandoned neutrality. On October 9, 1941, the president urged Congress to lift the "crippling provisions" of the Neutrality Act, permit the arming of merchant vessels, and allow them to enter combat zones.[312] America First, as Cole explains, campaigned against the bill arguing that the repeal of such major provisions of the Neutrality Act put the country into war.[313] Under the impression of the attacks on *USS Kearny* and *Reuben James*, the Congress agreed to the proposal in relatively close votes in mid-November 1941, as Doenecke reports.[314] The 1939 neutrality act was dead. According to Dallek, FDR, however, knew that winning the congressional approval for going to war would need a substantial provocation.[315] The Japanese attack on Pearl Harbor on December 7, 1941, followed by Hitler's declaration of war against the United States solved the president's dilemma. The country was at war. Consequently, as Cole writes, the America First Committee voted for a complete dissolution of the organization on December 11, 1941; the members agreed that the primary objective for the nation would now be victory.[316] Isolationist opposition to entanglement in European affairs had come to an end.

---

[310] Cole, *America First*, 161.
[311] Dallek, *Franklin D. Roosevelt and American Foreign Policy*, 291.
[312] United States Department of State, *Peace and War*, 762–63.
[313] Cole, *America First*, 163.
[314] Doenecke, *Storm on the Horizon*, 268.
[315] Dallek, *Franklin D. Roosevelt and American Foreign Policy*, 292.
[316] Cole, *America First*, 194–95.

III. DEALING WITH A NEW RESPONSIBILITY—U.S. FOREIGN POLICY AFTER THE SECOND WORLD WAR

The years after the Second World War marked a fundamental transformation in U.S. foreign policy toward Europe. Although the United States had involved itself in two wars within the last three decades, notions of non-entanglement in European affairs, following the dictum of the Monroe Doctrine, had always been strong. After the First World War, the United States eschewed membership in the League of Nations and returned to a policy of isolation. The Roosevelt administration had to convince the reluctant American public to go to war and confronted strong resistance from within the Congress and potent interest groups, which only abandoned resistance for the sake of war. Following the guiding principles of U.S. foreign policy, the United States should have resumed a focus on its domestic problems and should have brought back the troops from Europe; instead, the Americans fundamentally changed their policy and implemented a new internationalism. In the immediate years after the war and in the decades thereafter, this step was not unchallenged.

A. The Path to NATO—U.S. Responsibility for European Security

In 1949, with a gentle pressure from the Europeans, the United States became the leader of NATO. This section analyzes the process and arguments behind why the Americans threw the last constraint—entanglement in permanent alliances, an issue manifested in Washington's Farewell Address[317]—overboard, which finally led to full military involvement in European security affairs.

---

[317] For further details, see Appendix.

1. Historical Overview

The United States emerged from the Second World War as an economic and military superpower. During the war, as Herring recaps, production capacities tripled and made the Unites States the largest economic power in the world; additionally, America possessed atomic weapons and had 12.5 million people under arms, which made it so difficult for the Truman administration to change from wartime to peacetime economy without causing immense domestic political turmoil.[318] In Europe, the United Kingdom and France lost their great power status and suffered from severe economic problems and internal and external security challenges due to an emerging communist threat, which encouraged them to call for economic and military help from the Americans.[319] The 1947 Truman Doctrine and the Marshall Plan, according to historian Lawrence S. Kaplan, were the first steps toward an economic stabilization of Western Europe, but it soon turned out that a transatlantic security arrangement was necessary.[320] In April 1948, the Brussels Treaty between Great Britain, France, and the Benelux became the role model for a regional security alliance. It was necessary, though, to convince U.S. isolationists that such a pact would be in the country's interest. Finally, the Senate's 1948 Vandenberg Resolution cleared the way for negotiations leading to the signing of the North Atlantic Treaty in 1949.[321] According to Kaplan, the European NATO members needed extensive military aid, and desired the mingling of material support with the treaty, which upset American isolationists since it increased the risk of a dilution of European defense efforts.[322] Herring explains that the National Security Council Report 68 (NSC-68) in early 1950 called for a massive increase of U.S. defense efforts to counter the growing Soviet threat, and, in June 1950, the North Korean attack on its southern neighbor triggered a fundamental

---

[318] Herring, *From Colony to Superpower*, 597–98.

[319] Ibid., 596-97.

[320] Lawrence S. Kaplan, *The United States and NATO: The Formative Years* (Lexington: University Press of Kentucky, 1984), 49.

[321] Herring, *From Colony to Superpower*, 625.

[322] Kaplan, *United States and NATO*, 122.

reorientation of U.S. foreign policy toward Europe.[323] According to Kaplan, the Korean War raised the fear that Europe would fall under Soviet control immediately; the United States needed to strengthen NATO.[324] In late 1950, as a result of this policy change, President Harry S. Truman announced the sending of U.S. troops to Europe not knowing that he would spark a broad congressional dispute about constitutional competences and the scope of U.S. military commitments to Europe—the Great Debate. This debate went on until April 1951, when the Senate finally ended its resistance to Truman's new policy. Criticism, however, would persist.

2. September 1945 to December 1947—U.S. Domestic Political Situation and the Emergence of the Cold War

With the end of the Second World War in September 1945, the United States had to transition from wartime to peacetime economy. During the war, according to historian Warren I. Cohen, millions of black Americans had been drawn to the factories, and women had taken jobs that were traditionally held by men. Now, with the end of the war, the United States confronted a slump in demand for war materials, and millions of young men flooded the labor market due to demobilization, which caused severe structural and social tensions.[325] "If there was ever a time to put America first, this was it," Cohen writes.[326] In sum, the transition to a capable peacetime economy became the top priority.

To solve the crisis, according to David McCullough, Truman presented his 21-point domestic program to Congress on September 6, 1945. The program envisaged social benefits such as increased unemployment compensation, an increase in the minimum wage, or tax reforms; however, the proposal confronted stiff resistance for being

---

[323] Herring, *From Colony to Superpower*, 638–39.

[324] Kaplan, *United States and NATO*, 148–49.

[325] Warren I. Cohen, *The Cambridge History of American Foreign Relations: America in the Age of Soviet Power, 1945–1991* (New York: Cambridge University Press, 1993), 22.

[326] Ibid., 23.

more ambitious than FDR's New Deal.[327] In his address to Congress, Truman said,

> The major objective, of course, is to reestablish an expanded [U.S.] peacetime industry, trade, and agriculture, and to do it as quickly as possible. ... We have a moral obligation to the people of these liberated areas [Europe]. ... Hungry people are rarely advocates of democracy. The rehabilitation of these countries, and indeed the removal of American occupational troops, may be unnecessarily delayed if we fail to meet these responsibilities during the next few months.[328]

In other words, Truman's plan was clear from the very beginning: revitalize the domestic economy, provide economic support for Europe, promote democracy, and implement a withdrawal of the U.S. troops from Europe. Thus, he planned to follow the U.S. tradition of immediate disentanglement from the costly European adventure.

Truman's inability to solve the economic problems had severe political consequences during the mid-term congressional election. In 1946, as McCullough explains, the labor situation grew steadily worse, and strikes in the steel, railroad, and mining industry as well as an unpopular price control policy caused a drop in the president's approval rating from 82 percent in 1945 to 32 percent in September 1946.[329] The congressional elections in November 1946 largely became a referendum on Truman's domestic policy.

Herring writes that the power-hungry Republicans, who were in the opposition since 1932, wanted to regain control over the Congress and the White House—and Truman's unpopularity boosted their results, enabling them to gain a stunning victory in both houses.[330] In the new

---

[327] David McCullough, *Truman* (New York: Simon & Schuster, 1992), 468–69.

[328] Harry S. Truman, "Special Message to the Congress Presenting a 21-Point Program for the Reconversion Period," American Presidency Project, University of California, September 6, 1945, http://www.presidency.ucsb.edu/ws/?pid=12359.

[329] McCullough, *Truman*, 481, 498, 506, 520–21.

[330] Herring, *From Colony to Superpower*, 598-99.

80th Congress, Senator Arthur Hendrick Vandenberg of Michigan became the chairman of the Foreign Relations Committee, and Senator Robert Alphonso Taft of Ohio attended to domestic issues. McCullough writes that Vandenberg had been an all-out isolationist before the war, but witnessing a German V1 rocket attack on London had changed his mind; Senator Taft, on the other hand, was a hardcore isolationist, had little regard for Truman, and saw his purpose in opposing the president's policy.[331] In other words, Vandenberg would take a mediating position in foreign political affairs, whereas Taft had isolationist ambitions, which he would intertwine with domestic political issues.

The major foreign political challenge was the rise of Communism in Europe. At the Yalta Conference in February 1945, as Trachtenberg explains, the Western allies and the Soviet Union agreed upon spheres of influence, which should allow Poland democratic elections and a certain amount of autonomy.[332] The Soviets, however, did not intend to honor their commitments. In April 1945, the Soviets imposed a Communist police state on Poland. Trachtenberg writes that, although the United States did not welcome the Soviet course, it finally recognized the new Polish government, which indicated that the Americans were not willing to fight for democracy elsewhere in Europe.[333] By the time of the Potsdam Conference in July 1945, as Herring writes, the Soviets were pushing their influence outward in the Middle East, the Mediterranean, and in Eastern Europe, which was a "litmus test of Soviet postwar behavior."[334] A stable postwar settlement with the Soviet Union seemed out of range.

Aggressive Soviet policy required an adjustment of U.S. political conduct vis-à-vis the Soviet Union. On February 9, 1946, Soviet leader Joseph Stalin warned of capitalism as a new source of general crisis and military conflicts and called for an increase in industrial production to

---

[331] McCullough, *Truman*, 530–31.

[332] Marc Trachtenberg, *A Constructed Peace: The Making of the European Settlement 1945–1963* (Princeton, NJ: Princeton University Press, 1999), 9–10.

[333] Ibid., 13.

[334] Herring, *From Colony to Superpower*, 601.

supply the Red Army against the enemy.[335] Less than two weeks later, on February 22, 1946, the U.S. *charge d'affaires* in Moscow Kennan wrote his famous 8,000-word Long Telegram, warning that for the Soviets with the United States "there can be no permanent *modus vivendi* that it is desirable and necessary that the internal harmony of our society be disrupted, our traditional way of life be destroyed, the international authority of our state be broken, if Soviet power is to be secure."[336] With the Long Telegram Kennan laid out the foundation of his containment policy.[337]

On March 5, 1946, former British Prime Minister Sir Winston Churchill held his famous Iron Curtain Speech at Westminster College in Fulton, Missouri, in which he explained that Eastern and Central Europe was subject to an "increasing measure of control from Moscow. ... There is nothing for which they [the Soviets] have less respect than for weakness, especially military weakness. ... If the Western Democracies stand together in strict adherence to the principles of the United Nations (UN) Charter, ... no one is likely to molest them."[338] Churchill called for a Western military alliance to contain Soviet expansionism.

The economic situation hampered the possibility for the Western Europeans to resist the communist threat. The harsh winter of 1946–1947 and a following summer drought, as Wallace J. Thies asserts, caused the economic recovery in Western Europe to come to a halt, endangering the European democratization process and giving rise to

---

[335] Joseph Stalin, "Stalin Election Speech," Seventeen Moments in Soviet History, Michigan State University, February 9, 1946, http://soviethistory.msu.edu/1947-2/cold-war/cold-war-texts/stalin-election-speech/.

[336] George F. Kennan, "Long Telegram," National Security Archive, George Washington University, February 22, 1946, http://nsarchive.gwu.edu/coldwar/documents/episode-1/kennan.htm.

[337] For further details, see Appendix.

[338] Winston Churchill, "The Sinews of Peace," International Churchill Society, March 5, 1946, http://www.winstonchurchill.org/resources/speeches/1946-1963-elder-statesman/120-the-sinews-of-peace.

communist movements.³³⁹ For instance, Alan Bullock notes that the French and Italian Communist Parties tried to increase their influence by disruptive strikes and protests against "American imperialism" to sabotage economic recovery.³⁴⁰ According to David Yost, in 1948, the Soviets regretted that they had not liberated France and Italy to assist the communist parties in gaining power.³⁴¹ The internal decay of the political system created a severe threat to the European democratization process.

Furthermore, as John Baylis points out, Britain was unable to contain the Soviet expansion in the Mediterranean and the Middle East.³⁴² For instance, as Timothy P. Ireland writes, on April 1, 1947, Britain called for U.S. support to assist the Greek monarchy against communist insurgents and to help Turkey in modernizing the army and resist Soviet political pressure.³⁴³ The U.S. answer was the Truman Doctrine, which—according to President Truman—showed that America was "willing to help free peoples to maintain their free institutions and their national integrity against aggressive movements that seek to impose upon them totalitarian regimes."³⁴⁴ Following the Truman Doctrine, the United States became involved in the Greek Civil War and later sent military aid and a 450-man advisory group, which became a role model for future interventions, Herring asserts.³⁴⁵ Thus, the Truman Doctrine had implications far beyond the actual crises in Greece and

---

339 Wallace J Thies, *Why NATO Endures* (New York: Cambridge University Press, 2009), 93–94.

340 Alan Bullock, *Ernest Bevin: Foreign Secretary 1945-1951* (New York: W.W. Norton, 1983), 487–88.

341 David S. Yost, *NATO's Balancing Act* (Washington: United States Institute of Peace, 2014), 3.

342 John Baylis, *The Diplomacy of Pragmatism* (Basingstoke: Palgrave Macmillan, 1993), 63.

343 Timothy P. Ireland, *Creating the Entangling Alliance: The Origins of the North Atlantic Treaty Organization* (Westport: Greenwood, 1981), 24.

344 Harry S. Truman, "Address Before a Joint Session of Congress," Avalon Project, Lillian Goldman Law Library, Yale Law School, March 12, 1947, http://avalon.law.yale.edu/20th_century/trudoc.asp.

345 Herring, *From Colony to Superpower*, 616.

Turkey since it marked the beginning of U.S. involvement in European affairs in the postwar world.

Europe needed a more general recovery plan since the Truman Doctrine was not enough. On April 29, 1947, as Ireland reports, the Joint Chiefs of Staff stressed the importance of Western Europe for U.S. security. Furthermore, they emphasized that the main threat to Europe was of a political and not military nature; hence, Undersecretary of State Dean Gooderham Acheson linked the recovery of Europe to the fate of Germany and ordered the Policy Planning Staff to develop a plan for European recovery.[346] On June 5, 1947, Secretary of State George Marshall presented the outcome of the planning process and explained that the Europeans needed "substantial additional help or face economic, social, and political deterioration of a very grave character."[347]

According to Thies, the Americans believed that with the help of a strong economy Europe would be able to regain military strength and care for its own security; the European Recovery Program, known as the Marshall Plan, then would provide billions of dollars to revitalize European economy.[348] In sum, it became clear that U.S. foreign policy would prioritize economic recovery instead of military help—as Truman had envisaged before Congress in September 1945.

3. December 1947 to March 1948—The Brussels Pact

Western Europe needed a new security arrangement because the Soviet blockade policy made European division inevitable. According to Cees Wiebes and Bert Zeeman, the London Conference in December 1947 destroyed the last hopes for a security arrangement with the Soviet Union since the occupation powers could not agree on a joint policy for

---

[346] See Ireland, *Creating the Entangling Alliance*, 33–36.

[347] George C. Marshall, "The 'Marshall Plan' Speech," Organization for Economic Cooperation and Development, June 5, 1947, http://www.oecd.org/general/themarshallplanspeechatharvarduniversity5june1947.htm.

[348] Thies, *Why NATO Endures*. 94–95.

Germany.[349] As a result, as Young asserts, Britain and France immediately emphasized the need for a security alliance with the United States to contain communism.[350] In early January 1948, Britain was convinced that Western Europe would need a formal or informal arrangement, which should include the United States, Canada, Italy, Greece, the Scandinavian countries, Portugal, and—as soon as possible—Spain and Germany, Baylis reports.[351] According to Ireland, such a treaty should follow the lines of the 1946 Anglo-French Treaty of Dunkirk, which aimed at preventing German *revanchism*.[352] In sum, the first impulse for a transatlantic alliance came from the European side.

The nature of the British plan baffled the United States. On January 19, 1948, as Ireland explains, the Director of the Office of European Affairs John Hickerson raised concerns about the Dunkirk model proposal since, in the future, Germany would play a major role in European security: Germany could not forever be an enemy.[353] Kennan, now the State Department's Director of Policy Planning, argued that an economic build-up and a political union should be achieved first.[354]

Kaplan reports that Secretary Marshall welcomed the British proposal but did not want a public pronouncement of his support.[355] Still, the U.S. official line adhered to the goals of the Marshall Plan—stability through economic prosperity—especially since Marshall, as Wiebes and Zeeman write, did not want to endanger the congressional approval of the European Recovery Plan.[356] Isolationists, according to Kaplan, welcomed any European security arrangement directed against

---

[349] Cees Wiebes and Bert Zeeman, "The Pentagon Negotiations March 1948: The Launching of the North Atlantic Treaty," *International Affairs* 59, no. 3 (1983): 352.

[350] John W. *Young, Britain, France, and the Unity of Europe, 1945-1951* (Leicester: Leicester University Press, 1984), 78.

[351] Baylis, *Diplomacy of Pragmatism*, 66.

[352] Ireland, *Creating the Entangling Alliance*, 63.

[353] Ibid., 64.

[354] See Kaplan, *United States and NATO*, 59.

[355] Lawrence S. Kaplan, *The United States and NATO: The Formative Years* (Lexington: University Press of Kentucky, 1984), 51.

[356] Wiebes and Zeeman, "Pentagon Negotiations," 353.

the Soviet Union as a trade-off for the Marshall Plan aid, which would enable a U.S. troop withdrawal from Europe; furthermore, a united Europe could be potent trade partner.[357] On January 20, 1948, Republican Foreign Affairs advisor John Foster Dulles announced that a European alliance should follow the model of a regional pact under Article 51 of the UN Charter—similar to the Pan-American Rio Pact that the United States had recently signed.[358] Hickerson, however, stressed on the following day, that the initiative for any U.S. involvement must come from the European side.[359] In short, the United States slowly abandoned its resistance to an alliance with the Western European partners.

Britain pushed the idea of a transatlantic partnership forward. On January 22, 1948, British Foreign Secretary Ernest Bevin announced in an address to the British House of Commons, "The free nations of Western Europe must now draw closely together. ... We shall not be diverted ... from our aim of uniting by trade, social, cultural, and all other contacts those nations of Europe and of the world who are ready and able to cooperate."[360] Bullock explains that Bevin let his speech settle for a few days and, on January 26, 1948, tried to obtain a definite commitment of U.S. involvement in the defense of Europe.[361] The Americans, however, denied his request.

On February 7, 1948, according to Ireland, Undersecretary of State Robert Lovett explained that it would be unwise to initiate further military and political commitments since the Marshall Plan was presented to Congress as an option to help Europe back on its feet and reduce the long-range costs for the United States.[362] Kaplan stresses that the

---

[357] Kaplan, *United States and NATO*, 54.

[358] See Ibid., 52.

[359] See Ireland, *Creating the Entangling Alliance*, 65.

[360] Ernest Bevin, "Address Given to the House of Commons," University of Luxembourg, January 22, 1948, 11, http://www.cvce.eu/content/publication/2002/9/9/7bc0ecbd-c50e-4035-8e36-ed70bfbd204c/publishable_en.pdf.

[361] Bullock, *Ernest Bevin*, 522.

[362] Ireland, *Creating the Entangling Alliance*, 66.

Americans signaled that an alliance with Western Europe was premature, and that the Europeans should organize themselves before receiving any help.³⁶³ The United States wanted proof of Europe's willingness to take responsibility for their security.

The Czech Crisis accelerated decision-making. On February 19, 1948, Kaplan points out, Belgium and the Netherlands made a counterproposal to the Anglo-French Dunkirk model and emphasized an economic, political, and military regional organization in conformity with Article 51 of the UN Charter—exactly as the Americans recommended.³⁶⁴ In late February 1948, the Czech crisis erupted, ultimately showing that Europe was not able to defend itself against internal and external threats. Secretary Marshall announced on February 28, 1948, that the French desire for security against Germany and the containment of the Soviet Union were closely linked, and the United States would offer sustained security guarantees as long as the Soviet threat was acute.³⁶⁵ Marshall's promise broke French resistance, and on March 17, 1948, the parties signed the Brussels Treaty "to fortify and preserve the principles of democracy, personal freedom and political liberty, the constitutional traditions and the rule of law."³⁶⁶ Furthermore, the treaty emphasized the need "to strengthen ... the economic, social and cultural ties," and collaborate "in economic, social and cultural matters, and ... collective self-defense."³⁶⁷ Within a few weeks, the Europeans had created an alliance based on Western liberal democratic principles and economic and security collaboration, which was the prerequisite for an American entanglement in the defense of Europe.

---

363 Kaplan, *United States and NATO*, 59.
364 Ibid., 60.
365 See Ireland, *Creating the Entangling Alliance*, 69.
366 North Atlantic Treaty Organization, *NATO Basic Documents* (Brussels: NATO Information Service, 1976), 8.
367 Ibid.

4. March 1948 to April 1949—The Path to NATO

With the help of the Czech crisis, Bevin pressed the United States to attach itself to Western Europe. According to Ireland, the British foreign minister submitted three concepts of a future transatlantic agreement: an Anglo-French-Benelux alliance with U.S. backing, a close alliance with the United States, and a Mediterranean security system with a special focus on Italy.[368] On March 11, 1948, Hickerson indicated that the United States preferred participation in a North Atlantic-Mediterranean regional defense arrangement according to Articles 51 and 52 of the UN Charter to begin on March 15, 1948.[369] On the following day, Marshall informed Bevin that the United States was prepared to start negotiations on the establishment of an Atlantic security system immediately.[370] On March 17, 1948, the day of the signing of the Brussels Treaty, President Truman announced before Congress, "I am sure that the determination of the free countries of Europe to protect themselves will be matched by an equal determination on our part. ... We keep our occupation forces in Germany until the peace is secure in Europe."[371] The United States was ready for a greater Western alliance.

Isolationist sentiments hampered the negotiation process. According to Wiebes and Zeeman, negotiations between the United States, Canada, and Great Britain started on March 22, 1948, and, within a week, the delegations reached consensus over the scope of a Western alliance and agreed that negotiations on a Security Pact for the North Atlantic region should start in May.[372] During the negotiations, according to Kaplan, the Americans hesitated to make binding commitments, which caused some fear among the partners that the United States might fall back into prewar isolationism, which encouraged a Canadian delegate to quip, "If you scratch almost any American long enough, you will

---

[368] Ireland, *Creating the Entangling Alliance*, 72.

[369] See Kaplan, *United States and NATO*, 62.

[370] See Bullock, *Ernest Bevin*, 530.

[371] Harry S. Truman, "Special Message to the Congress on the Threat to the Freedom of Europe," American Presidency Project, University of California, March 17, 1948, http://www.presidency.ucsb.edu/ws/?pid=13130.

[372] Wiebes and Zeeman, "Pentagon Negotiations," 361.

find an isolationist. They suffer ... from a homesickness for isolation."[373]

According to Thomas, Kennan still insisted on the strict political nature of any treaty with the Europeans; instead of a military alliance, he opted for arms deliveries to Western Europe—similar to the U.S. policy before both world wars.[374] Ireland asserts that, besides facing some resistance from individuals within in the State Department, the plans also needed congressional endorsement.[375] Wiebes and Zeeman point out that the State Department conducted intensive talks with Senator Vandenberg to line up Congress behind the idea of an Atlantic alliance.[376] Resolution 239, the so-called Vandenberg Resolution, passed the Senate on June 11, 1948, and recommended an "association of the United States, by constitutional process, with such regional and other collective arrangements as are based on continuous and effective self-help and mutual aid, and as affect its national security."[377] In sum, the Congress demanded a say in the treaty process and also expressed concerns that the Europeans needed to share the burden of the defense of Europe—a herald of future debates. The Vandenberg Resolution, however, ended the resistance within the State Department and the way was free for further negotiations.

During the further negotiation process of the North Atlantic Treaty, political opposition formed for various reasons. Kaplan asserts that a major factor for U.S. hesitation was European insensitivity toward isolationist traditions and the role of the legislative branch in the making of U.S. foreign policy as well as the coming presidential election in November 1948.[378] Concerning the two former points, the greatest obstacle was Article V of the treaty, which demanded mutual assistance if

---

[373] Quoted in Kaplan, *United States and NATO*, 75.

[374] Ian, Q. R Thomas, *The Promise of Alliance: NATO and the Political Imagination* (Lanham, MD: Rowman & Littlefield, 1997), 12; see also Wiebes and Zeeman, "Pentagon Negotiations," 362.

[375] Ireland, *Creating the Entangling Alliance*, 80–81.

[376] Wiebes and Zeeman, "Pentagon Negotiations," 363.

[377] North Atlantic Treaty Organization, *NATO Basic Documents*, 11.

[378] Kaplan, *United States and NATO*, 87.

one member was under attack. Ireland concludes that the Europeans wanted a binding formula with automatic guarantees, whereas the Americans preferred not to make any specific concessions.[379] The U.S. line followed the Farewell Address' tradition of avoiding binding alliances.

The other important issue was the presidential election in November 1948, in which Republican candidate Thomas E. Dewey of New York was highly favored. Cohen writes that Truman defeated Dewey just because of the successful U.S. airlift as an answer to the Berlin Blockade (June 1948 to May 1949), which demonstrated American might and countered criticism of Truman being too soft on communism.[380] Truman's surprise victory angered rank-and-file Republicans, who now pressed for an end to bipartisanship in foreign policy and demanded an orchestrated savage attack on the president's policy.[381] Foreign policy was a huge playing field on which to do so.

The obligations of Article V became the focus of the political debates. According to Ireland, the initial draft of the Transatlantic Treaty, completed on December 24, 1948, included an automatic commitment that in case of an armed attack each member would take "forthwith such military or other action, individually and in concert with the other Parties, as may be necessary to restore and assure the security of the North Atlantic Area."[382] This proposal quickly ran into trouble with the Senate. In early February 1949, the new chairman of the Foreign Relations Committee, Senator Thomas Terry Connally of Texas, and Senator Vandenberg demanded a more "neutral language" in Article V and even questioned the phrasing "that an attack on one would be considered an attack on all."[383]

According to Acheson, the administration confronted a dilemma because the more vaguely it phrased Article V, the more likely the oppo-

---

[379] Ireland, *Creating the Entangling Alliance*, 106.
[380] Cohen, *America in the Age of Soviet Power*, 48.
[381] See Ibid., 50.
[382] Ireland, *Creating the Entangling Alliance*, 110.
[383] Ibid., 110–11.

sition would agree, but the less likely the article would fulfill its purpose.[384] Finally, the senators agreed to add the phrase "such action as each deems necessary, including the use of armed force."[385] The tempest over Article V calmed down and the way was open for the signature of the treaty on April 4, 1949.

5. April 1949 to June 1950—Implementing the Treaty and the Military Aid Program

The North Atlantic Treaty, especially Article III with its two objectives of self-help and mutual assistance, came under close examination by the Congress. This scrutiny was sparked on April 5, 1949, just one day after the signing of the treaty, when the Brussels Pact Powers requested military aid from the United States. Kaplan concludes that this move clearly indicated the major preoccupation of the Europeans with material help, which for many U.S. senators was a proof that Europe simply wanted to drain the United States.[386]

Consequently, some senators, among them Senator Taft, believed—as Kennan did—that the treaty should not contain any military obligations beyond political guarantees, Ireland writes.[387] According to Phil Williams, isolationists were upset over intertwining military aid with the guarantees of the treaty. In the end, 21 senators, among them Taft, supported a reservation—finally defeated—preventing any military assistance based on Article III; their voters would not accept a tax increase to arm Western Europe, they argued.[388] Vandenberg, as Kaplan points out, feared "that the introduction of the Military Assistance Bill ... would present the Treaty in the wrong light," and therefore he proposed a decoupling of the discussions over the treaty and the military

---

[384] Dean Acheson, *Present at the Creation: My Years in the State Department* (New York: Norton, 1969), 280.
[385] Ibid., 281.
[386] Kaplan, *United States and NATO*, 121.
[387] Ireland, *Creating the Entangling Alliance*, 120.
[388] Phil Williams, *The Senate and U.S. Troops in Europe* (New York: St. Martin's, 1985), 26–27.

aid program.[389] In other words, the administration needed to obfuscate in the debate about Article III during the Senate hearings.

During a hearing on April 27, 1949, Acheson explained that the treaty would follow the lines of the Monroe Doctrine. According to Ireland, the secretary thereby "succeeded in invoking the shibboleths of isolationism to win acceptance of a policy that marked the departure from isolationist traditions.[390] Senator Bourke Hickenlooper of Iowa asked Acheson if the United States was "going to be expected to send substantial numbers of troops over there as a more or less permanent contribution," to which Acheson answered with a decisive "No."[391] This statement would become important during the Senate hearings in 1951.

On July 9, 1949, Vandenberg announced his support for the treaty. He explained that the treaty was a "literal departure from orthodox American diplomacy," but it did not depart from "a philosophy of preventive action against aggression," which was in line with the Monroe Doctrine, and the arming of Europe would not be the purpose of the treaty.[392]

Kaplan writes that the foes of the North Atlantic treaty criticized the United States for associating with countries against which the 1823 Monroe Doctrine originally was directed, and they opposed engaging in any form of alliance—in the tradition of the Farewell Address— since it would limit the country's freedom of action.[393] Instead, as Taft proposed on July 11, 1949, the United States should simply extend the Monroe Doctrine to Western Europe.[394] Although the doubts about the treaty and military assistance program remained unresolved, the

---

[389] Kaplan, *United States and NATO*, 122.

[390] Ireland, *Creating the Entangling Alliance*, 121.

[391] United States Senate, Committee on Foreign Relations, *First Session on Executive L, the North Atlantic Treaty. Part I: Administration Witnesses, United States Senate*, 81st Cong., 1st sess. (Washington, DC: GPO, 1949), 47.

[392] See Ireland, *Creating the Entangling Alliance*, 145–46.

[393] Lawrence S. Kaplan, *Recent American Foreign Policy: Conflicting Interpretations* (Homewood, IL: Dorsey, 1968), 94.

[394] Ibid.

Senate followed Vandenberg's proposal and overwhelmingly supported the North Atlantic Treaty on July 21, 1949, which constituted a vote of confidence for a major shift in U.S. foreign policy, as Kaplan explains.[395] Nevertheless, the Senate approved the treaty under very narrow conditions: neither should there be any binding military commitments, nor should the United States send troops to Europe.

The disillusionment came only four days afterward, when the president sent a proposal for providing military assistance to the European partners. Acheson writes that the initial request asked for $1.4 billion and immediately caused a congressional revolt by isolationists such as Taft and Vandenberg, who argued that such a bill "would permit the President to sell, lease or give away anything ... to any country ... [and] would make him the number one war lord of the earth."[396] In essence, Truman was asking for a boundless Lend-Lease act, as FDR did in 1941.

Furthermore, isolationists believed that the Europeans wanted to load the burden of the defense of Europe upon the United States, Kaplan asserts.[397] For instance, Vandenberg believed that the treaty was sufficient to deter the Soviets, and that there was no need for a military aid program.[398] As a response to the Senate reservations, on August 5, 1949, the president submitted a new bill limiting the scope of the program to NATO members. He failed, though, to address Vandenberg's deterrence concern. This failure, as Acheson points out, encouraged the senator to propose a limitation on any aid unless the North Atlantic Council (NAC) presented a concrete defense strategy that could be approved by Congress.[399] By January 6, 1950, according to historian Gregory W. Pedlow, the NAC produced a formal defense plan yielding a force, which was based on labor division between the members capable of containing a Soviet invasion. The United States

---

[395] Kaplan, *Recent American Foreign Policy*, 95.

[396] See Acheson, *Present at the Creation*, 309.

[397] Kaplan, *United States and NATO*, 128.

[398] See Ireland, *Creating the Entangling Alliance*, 154.

[399] Acheson, *Present at the Creation*, 310–11.

was responsible for strategic bombing, and the Europeans would provide tactical air support and the majority of the ground forces—with France providing the core of ground troops.[400] The NAC had provided the formal conditions for the military aid program.

The Senate still had doubts about the soundness of the NATO plans. Ireland reveals that Vandenberg had little faith in French military capabilities as a first line of defense in Europe; Dulles shared this view and saw West Germany as the key for security in Europe.[401] According to Acheson, several attempts followed in the Senate to reduce the actual numbers of the financial aid; finally, however, the Military Assistance Program passed the Senate by a vote of 55 to 24.[402] Ireland writes that the first successful test of a Soviet atomic bomb on August 29, 1949 (announced by Truman on September 23) helped to pass the bill.[403] Williams points out that the debates about the military implementation of the North Atlantic Treaty erased bipartisanship in U.S. foreign affairs; furthermore, the treaty text was vague about responsibilities, and the Soviet nuclearization nullified the deterrence effect of U.S. atomic weapons, bringing conventional defense to the forefront.[404] The administration had reached its goals but would have to pay a high price.

The United States needed to update its defense strategy because of the new Soviet threat. In 1950, as Paul H. Nitze and S. Nelson Drew explain, the envisaged U.S. defense budget was $13.5 billion, but Truman wanted cuts of nearly 50 percent because of the poor economy.[405] Acheson writes that, given the foreign political circumstances, especially the Soviet nuclearization, the president ordered the policy planning staff under Kennan's successor, Paul H. Nitze, on January 31,

---

[400] Gregory W. Pedlow, "NATO Strategy Documents 1949-1969," Historical Office, Supreme Headquarters Allied Powers Europe, 1999, XIII, http://www.nato.int/docu/stratdoc/eng/intro.pdf.

[401] Ireland, *Creating the Entangling Alliance*, 156.

[402] Acheson, *Present at the Creation*, 312.

[403] Ireland, *Creating the Entangling Alliance*, 157; Truman signed the bill on October 6, 1949.

[404] Williams, *Senate and U.S. Troops in Europe*, 33–34.

[405] Paul H. Nitze, S. Nelson Drew, and National Defense University, *NSC-68: Forging the Strategy of Containment* (Washington: National Defense University, 1994), 3.

1950, to review the current defense policy.[406] National Security Council document NSC-68, presented to Truman on April 25, 1950, concludes, "There exists a sharp disparity between our actual military strength and our commitments ... Our military strength is becoming dangerously inadequate," which requires "a level of military readiness, which can be maintained as long as necessary as a deterrent to Soviet aggression."[407]

Nitze and Drew explain that, in contrast to Kennan's containment policy expressed in his 1947 "X" article and laid down in earlier strategic documents, NSC-68 recommended substantially higher levels of defense efforts through strengthening the military instead of providing economic assistance to the allies.[408] According to Kaplan, NSC-68 did not include a cost estimation, but planners cautiously calculated annual costs of $50 billion, or 20 percent of the gross national product, almost four times the defense budget of 1950 without the proposed cuts.[409] Hence, Truman did not formally accept NSC-68, especially since "the aims and attitudes of the executive and legislative" diverged too much, Williams writes.[410] Acheson wanted a deeper U.S. entanglement in European security affairs, but for the Senate the financial burden had already reached the limit; in May and June 1950, "complacency rather than the urgency embodied in NSC-68 was the order of the day," Williams concludes.[411] The pressure was not yet high enough to convince the United States of the necessity for greater responsibility.

6. June 1950 to April 1951—The Great Debate

The invasion of South Korea changed the U.S. attitude about sending U.S. troops to Europe. Kaplan writes that the North Korean attack on its southern neighbor on June 25, 1950, convinced President Truman of a worldwide Communist conspiracy, and raised the fear of domino

---

[406] Acheson, *Present at the Creation*, 371.

[407] See full text of NSC-68 in Nitze, Drew, and National Defense University, *NSC-68*, 31, 65.

[408] Nitze, Drew, and National Defense University, *NSC-68*, 14–15.

[409] Kaplan, *United States and NATO*, 147.

[410] Williams, *Senate and U.S. Troops in Europe*, 35.

[411] Ibid.

effects similar to the prelude to the Second World War from 1936 to 1939 and 1941.[412] Within a few days, Truman decided to go to war. The question remained, though: what would the Soviets' next move be? What should be done about Germany and the European defense?

Williams writes that the NATO framework was still an empty shell that was incapable of preventing an attack similar to that in the Far East.[413] As a way to solve that problem, on July 31, 1950, Acheson proposed West Germany's rearmament and the integration of its military power into the framework of a European army, as Ireland states.[414] This approach, however, would need substantial U.S. troop commitments to Europe. Thus, on August 26, 1950, the president advised Acheson and Secretary of Defense Louis Johnson to develop a proposal, which Truman made public on September 9, 1950. He said:

> I have today approved substantial increases in the strength of the United States forces to be stationed in Western Europe in the interest of the defense of that area. ... A basic element in the implementation of this decision is the degree to which our friends match our actions in this regard. Firm programs for the development of their forces will be expected to keep full step with the dispatch of additional United States forces to Europe. Our plans are based on the sincere expectations that our efforts will be met with similar actions on their part.[415]

In other words, the United States expected that the European allies would take a fair share in the burden of European defense—the start of an everlasting debate in NATO. Finally, the provisions of NSC-68 would come into effect, but Truman needed congressional approval for his new policy. Given the 1947 Senate debates and the resistance against high financial commitments, this task would become extremely difficult.

---

[412] Kaplan, *United States and NATO*, 145, 148–49.
[413] Williams, *Senate and U.S. Troops in Europe*, 36.
[414] Ireland, *Creating the Entangling Alliance*, 190–91.
[415] Quoted in Williams, *Senate and U.S. Troops in Europe*, 37–38.

The mid-term congressional elections in November 1950 changed Truman's chance for the worse. Williams explains that foreign policy—except for Korea—played a relatively little role in the election; instead, the dominating themes were housing, employment, and education.[416] Nevertheless, the election had a significant impact on foreign policy because the Republicans won substantial gains and reduced the Democratic majority to two seats, which encouraged some Republican senators to criticize Truman's foreign policy more openly and abandon the traditional bipartisan approach in foreign affairs.[417] Furthermore, Senator Vandenberg, usually able to suppress criticism by the Midwest Republicans, was absent due to a fatal illness, which gave Taft the opportunity to end the division of labor between him and Vandenberg and increase his influence on the party's attitudes toward foreign relations.[418] Truman's plans for sending troops to Europe would confront strong opposition.

A blundering decision was to exclude the Congress from major decisions concerning NATO. By December 12, 1950, as Ireland points out, NATO approved the creation of a European Defense Force and recommended the establishment of a Supreme Headquarters Atlantic Powers in Europe (SHAPE) under the command of a U.S. officer.[419] During a NAC meeting in Brussels on December 17, 1950, Acheson announced that Truman had appointed General Dwight D. Eisenhower as the first supreme commander of NATO, and that the president would shortly increase U.S. troops in Europe under Eisenhower's command.[420] On December 22, 1950, Acheson reported on the results of the Brussels meeting in a foreign affairs committee hearing. Kaplan reports that this meeting sparked a Senate debate on January 5, 1951, in which Senator Taft complained that NATO's new role would unnecessarily enmesh the United States in European affairs, instead of

---

[416] Williams, *Senate and U.S. Troops in Europe*, 44.

[417] Ibid.

[418] Ibid.

[419] Ireland, *Creating the Entangling Alliance*, 207.

[420] See Ibid.

encouraging the Europeans to defend themselves.[421] Furthermore, Taft accused Truman for abusing his power and conducting a foreign policy harmful to national welfare. He said,

> We see now the beginning of an agreement to send a specified number of American troops to Europe without that question ever having been discussed in the Congress of the United States. ... There cannot be a bipartisan foreign policy unless it is a policy on which both parties agree. ... Republican minority cannot be attacked for failure to agree on policies on which they have not even been consulted or on policies which they may regard as detrimental to the welfare of the Nation.[422]

Acheson later described Taft's words as a "smashing attack against the whole internationalist position."[423] Henceforth, partisan policy and domestic policy would dominate the debates.

Furthermore, Taft stood under the impression of the Chinese Offensive in the Korean War (November 1950 to January 1951), which almost led to an entire disaster for the UN forces with heavy losses for the U.S. 8th Army, forcing it to retreat to a line well south of the 38th parallel.[424] Taft said, "I do not know ... whether we can maintain our position in Korea, but certainly we should not jeopardize our Army there to the extent of risking its destruction. ... I doubt if we should enter into any commitments ... unless we are sure it is well within our capacity."[425] In sum, as Williams writes, Taft's starting point for thinking about foreign affairs was the kind of America he wanted to see, and he feared that Truman's policy would result in the deconstruction of liberty and ruin the country.[426]

---

[421] Kaplan, *United States and NATO*, 165.

[422] 97 Cong. Rec. S60 (daily ed. Jan. 5, 1951).

[423] Acheson, *Present at the Creation*, 491.

[424] Richard W. Stewart, *The Korean War: The Chinese Intervention* (Washington: U.S. Army Center of Military History, 2000), 33.

[425] 97 Cong. Rec. S59 (daily ed. Jan. 5, 1951).

[426] Williams, *Senate and U.S. Troops in Europe*, 52–53.

As a result, the Senate started attacking the assignment of forces to NATO. On January 8, Senator Kenneth Wherry of Nebraska submitted a resolution stating that no U.S. ground forces should be assigned to NATO "pending determination by the Congress of a policy on that matter."[427] Wherry advocated an expanded air force—as Taft did—and proposed that the United States should surround Russia "with a ring of airbases."[428] Williams explains that Taft believed that only massive air power would deter the Russians, and ground forces would only provoke an attack; however, he accepted compromises since the United States had to fulfill the promised commitments to NATO.[429] Nevertheless, Taft warned that the formation of a great international army with the Americans in the lead would encourage the NATO allies to call constantly for the enlargement of U.S. presence in Europe.[430] In Taft's thinking, American domination in NATO would make U.S. "military presence ... more enduring and substantial than was either desirable or necessary," Williams concludes.[431] Hence, the debates in the following weeks would revolve around Wherry's resolution and Taft's ideas.

The first matter of discussion was the question of whether the president exceeded his authority in assigning forces to NATO. Truman immediately went on the offensive. In a press conference on January 11, 1951, he announced, "Under the President's constitutional powers as Commander in Chief of the Armed Forces he has the authority to send troops anywhere in the world. ... We will continue to send troops wherever it is necessary."[432] Obviously, Truman was convinced that he was acting within his constitutional authority, and a consultation of the

---

[427] 97 Cong. Rec. S94 (daily ed. Jan. 8, 1951).

[428] Ibid.

[429] Williams, *Senate and U.S. Troops in Europe*, 54.

[430] 97 Cong. Rec. S60 (daily ed. Jan. 5, 1951).

[431] See Williams, *Senate and U.S. Troops in Europe*, 55.

[432] Harry S. Truman, "The President's News Conference," American Presidency Project, University of California, January 11, 1951, http://www.presidency.ucsb.edu/ws/index.php?pid=14050.

Congress was just a matter of courtesy. According to Williams, Chairman Connally shared Truman's view; others such as Senator James P. Kem of Missouri argued that Truman turned the country into a military dictatorship.[433] Senator Wherry explained that the president was implementing the North Atlantic Treaty by indirection, creating facts under assumed constitutional authority, and sending troops although Congress' approval of Article III in 1949 referred to arms and not men.[434] Acheson's decisive "No" was going to backfire.

On January 17, 1951, Vandenberg wrote to Wherry that the Senate should recognize the president's authority, but any Senate resolution should emphasize the responsibility of Congress and urge the president to involve Congress in issues of Article III.[435] Williams writes that Senator Taft finally persuaded Wherry to relinquish a straight vote on his resolution because it would have been defeated; instead, Wherry should accept referral to a joint Armed Service and Foreign Relations Committee.[436] Truman, on the other hand, appreciated any positive resolution.[437] Nonetheless, it would be the task of the administration to convince a majority of the Senate of the need to send troops to Europe.

The second issue was the number and suitability of ground forces assigned to NATO, as well as burden sharing. During the hearings of the Senate Armed Services and Foreign Relations Committees on February 1, 1951, General Eisenhower emphasized the need for U.S. leadership since it would increase morale and inspire the Europeans by example.[438] He advised the committee not to fix the number of ground

---

[433] Williams, *Senate and U.S. Troops in Europe*, 64.

[434] 97 Cong. Rec. S325, S330 (daily ed. Jan. 16, 1951).

[435] See Ireland, *Creating the Entangling Alliance*, 211.

[436] Williams, *Senate and U.S. Troops in Europe*, 67.

[437] Harry S. Truman, "The President's News Conference," American Presidency Project, University of California, January 18, 1951, http://www.presidency.ucsb.edu/ws/index.php?pid=13843.

[438] United States Senate, Committee on Foreign Relations and Committee on Armed Services, *Assignment of Ground Forces of the United States to Duty in the European Area on S. Res. 8, United States Senate*, 82nd Cong., 1st sess. (Washington, DC: GPO, 1951), 22. Hereafter cited as *Assignment of Ground Forces*.

forces to a certain formula.⁴³⁹ Nonetheless, on February 8, 1951, as Williams writes, despite Eisenhower's reservation, Senator Taft made a proposal to introduce an arithmetic ratio of 1:9 of American to European forces, which should not exceed 20 percent of the total U.S. land and 10 percent of air force.⁴⁴⁰ Obviously, Eisenhower's testimony did not have the desired effect.

On February 14, 1951, 118 House Republicans advocated a "Declaration of Policy" stating that no aid should be provided to Western Europe unless it would carry the full share of the burden.⁴⁴¹ Representative Laurence Smith of Wisconsin commented on the proposal, "Government propaganda is beating the war drums again as it did in 1917 and in 1939. People are alarmed and confused. ... Since 1945 this Nation has been in the hands of Truman, Acheson, and Marshall. ... It is important that this Congress rise up and fight every measure which continues the present foreign policy."⁴⁴² Unabashed, Acheson informed the joint committee on the following day that the government envisaged sending four additional divisions to Europe, Ireland writes.⁴⁴³ The administration and Congress were at strife.

A battle between Senator Hickenlooper and Secretary Acheson revealed the core of the debate. On April 27, 1949, Acheson had testified before the Senate that the United States would not send troops to Western Europe under the provisions of Article III of the NATO treaty. During Acheson's hearing on February 16, 1951, Hickenlooper referred to the secretary's "No," but both ended in unproductive debates about how Acheson had understood the senator's question and how the testimony was meant.⁴⁴⁴ Williams reports that in 1949 the Senate had accepted Article III under very explicit assumptions, and that

---

⁴³⁹ *Assignment of Ground Forces*, 22.

⁴⁴⁰ Williams, *Senate and U.S. Troops in Europe*, 72

⁴⁴¹ 97 Cong. Rec. H1,258 (daily ed. Jan. 14, 1951).

⁴⁴² Ibid., H1,257–58.

⁴⁴³ Ireland, *Creating the Entangling Alliance*, 209.

⁴⁴⁴ *Assignment of Ground Forces*, 113–14.

now, since the nature of the commitment had changed, the administration should seek approval by Congress.[445] Both sides had to find an acceptable way of cooperation.

The solution was a new resolution to replace Senator Wherry's proposal. Williams explains that until the end of the hearings the members of the joint committee were unanimous in the issue of sending troops to Europe; nevertheless, there was consensus that they needed to draft an explicit approval of the administration's action.[446] On April 4, 1951, after several weeks of bitter debates, Senate Resolution 99 was brought to the floor to address the main themes of the Great Debate since December 1950.[447] The first and second paragraphs of the resolution approved the appointment of General Eisenhower and the principle of sending troops to Europe, placing them under Eisenhower's command as a U.S. contribution to the defense of the NATO area.[448] The Senate resolution also clearly stated the demand that the Europeans should take their share of the burden and "give full, realistic force and effect to the requirement of Article III, ... specifically insofar as the creation of combat units is concerned."[449] Paragraph 6 demands that any further assignment of troops under Article III—exceeding the proposed four divisions—would require congressional approval.[450] The Senate wanted to reestablish tight control.

The resolution passed the Senate by a vote of 45 to 41.[451] On April 11, the House defeated an attempt to include an amendment to the draft bill, which called for congressional approval for sending any troops to Europe.[452] According to Williams, this last attempt of the

---

[445] Williams, *Senate and U.S. Troops in Europe*, 81.

[446] Ibid.

[447] For the text of Senate Resolution 99 see 97 Cong. Rec. S3,282-3 (daily ed. Apr. 4, 1951); for details of the debates on Res. 99 see Williams, *Senate and U.S. Troops in Europe*, 98–107.

[448] 97 Cong. Rec. S3,282 (daily ed. Apr. 4, 1951).

[449] Ibid., S3,283.

[450] Ibid.

[451] 97 Cong. Rec. S3,293 (daily ed. Apr. 4, 1951).

[452] 97 Cong. Rec. H3,705 (daily ed. Apr. 11, 1951).

House ended the Great Debate; the Congress approved Truman's policy, demanded a great share in the decision-making over foreign policy, and did not see U.S. troops in Europe as an implicitness—especially under the light of fair burden sharing.[453] The United States had fully integrated itself in the defense of European security and had overcome its historic resistance to binding alliances. America, however, paid a high price because congressional bipartisanship in foreign policy affairs had faded away, and the desire for a fair burden sharing would remain one of the main concerns of U.S. policy toward NATO.

B. The Mansfield Resolutions—Opposition to High Levels of U.S. Troops in Europe

From the mid-1960s to the mid-1970s, the burden sharing debate came to the forefront again. Some U.S. senators, among them majority leader Michael J. Mansfield, argued that the European allies were not shouldering a fair share of European defense and demanded a significant reduction of U.S. troops in Europe. A series of Senate resolutions and amendments put severe pressure on the administration, but these attempts played into the hand of the Nixon administration, which occasionally used force reductions as a bargaining chip to convince the European allies to spend more for the defense of Europe. The United States, however, was playing a dangerous game. These domestic political power games between the Senate and the administration could have easily caused a major rift in the transatlantic partnership. Without the staunch support of some true Atlanticists such as President Nixon and his "Old Guard," Senate initiatives might have caused serious harm to NATO.

1. Historical Overview

The analysis of the opposition to large numbers of U.S. troops in Europe primarily focuses on the interplay between the Senate and the Johnson and Nixon administrations. This section provides a broader picture of the international and the domestic political situation, which

---

[453] Williams, *Senate and U.S. Troops in Europe*, 107.

should help to explain the motives of Mansfield and his fellow campaigners.

a. Challenges of the Vietnam War

The Vietnam War caused a rift between the president and Congress. The fall of 1963 and the first half of 1964 was a pivotal moment for the United States. Former Secretary of Defense Robert S. McNamara explains that the overthrow and the assassination of South Vietnam's President Ngo Dinh Diem confronted the United States with an unraveling political situation in Vietnam, which increased the demands for military action.[454] On August 2, 1964, a North Vietnamese torpedo boat attacked the destroyer *USS Maddox*, which led the Johnson administration to seek immediate congressional support for its Southeast Asia policy.[455] The Tonkin Gulf Resolution authorized the president to take "all necessary measures to repel any armed attack against the forces of the United States and to prevent further aggressions."[456] Congress had given the president a *carte blanche*. Johnson, then, unleashed a military intervention that included nearly 550,000 U.S. troops during the peak phase in 1968; according to McNamara, the Senate had never intended to send such numbers to Vietnam, and some senators believed that the president misused the "power bestowed by the resolution"—a phase one would later call the Imperial Presidency.[457] For instance, the Senators Fulbright and Mansfield accused the Johnson administration of having misled them during the hearings that preceded the 1964 Tonkin Gulf Resolution.[458] In 1967, the Senate Foreign Committee explained, "Congress committed the error of making a personal judge-

---

[454] Robert S. McNamara, *In Retrospect: The Tragedy and Lessons of Vietnam* (New York: Times Books, 1995), 100–1.

[455] Lyndon Baines Johnson, *The Vantage Point: Perspectives of the Presidency 1963-1969* (New York: Holt, Rinehart and Winston, 1971), 116.

[456] "Tonkin Gulf Resolution," 100 milestone documents, U.S. National Archives and Records Administration, January 7, 1964, https://ourdocuments.gov/doc.php?doc=98&page=transcript.

[457] McNamara, *In Retrospect*, 142.

[458] Ibid., 141–42.

ment ... as to what any President would do with so great an acknowledgement of power."⁴⁵⁹ These disputes about congressional versus presidential authority over the conduct of U.S. military foreign policy caused deep mistrust and were an underlying cause of Mansfield's crusade against the Johnson and Nixon administrations.

Since the United States suffered heavy losses during the Vietnam War, anti-militarism was on the rise. In February 1965, according to McNamara, 64 percent of the American people strongly backed the U.S. intervention in Vietnam, but these numbers soon changed dramatically.⁴⁶⁰ For instance, in November 1965, the young Quaker Norman R. Morrison burned himself to protest the loss of lives and human suffering in Vietnam; only three weeks later 35,000 people marched on the White House, and many more demonstrations followed.⁴⁶¹ Hence, the American public developed a strong aversion to the military, which influenced the debates about U.S. troop reductions in Europe. Williams, for example, explains that Mansfield received considerable amounts of mail of which the vast majority approved his initiatives and which may have encouraged him to carry on with his policy despite its being defeated several times.⁴⁶² Thus, the public was in favor of a more conservative policy toward U.S. troop contributions to Europe.

b. Economic Political Situation

From the mid-1960s until 1969 excessive spending by the Johnson administration caused high inflation. Samuel Rosenberg writes that, as a result of the Vietnam War, U.S. defense spending increased between the middle of 1965 and 1968 by more than 60 percent, or $30 billion.⁴⁶³ In parallel, as former U.S. President Lyndon Baines Johnson explains, public expenditures for education, health, employment, and poverty reduction—a result of the "Great Society" program—grew and raised

---

⁴⁵⁹ Quoted in McNamara, *In Retrospect*, 141.

⁴⁶⁰ Ibid., 173.

⁴⁶¹ Ibid., 216–17.

⁴⁶² Williams, *Senate and U.S. Troops in Europe*, 200.

⁴⁶³ Samuel Rosenberg, *American Economic Development since 1945* (Gordonsville, VA: Palgrave Macmillan, 2003), 114.

demand faster than production could follow.[464] According to Jeffry A. Frieden, neither the war expenditures nor the social welfare spending were very popular, so the Johnson administration abstained from raising taxes and instead increased deficit spending, which drove inflation in the United States higher than in many other partners.[465] In December 1965, as Rosenberg explains, the Federal Reserve (FED) implemented a restrictive monetary policy and raised the interest rates to cool down the market; in 1966, the FED reduced the money supply, which boosted interest rates dramatically.[466] Johnson explains that, as living costs rose, workers demanded higher wages, which increased production costs and caused higher prices; "I saw a dangerous inflation creeping in," he claims.[467] As Rosenberg writes, the FED's restrictive monetary policy caused only a minor slowdown of the economy, and in 1967 inflation accelerated again. This situation forced the Johnson administration to ask for a 10 percent income tax surcharge and cuts from nondefense expenditures that materialized in the Revenue and Expenditure Control Act of 1968; however, the measures came too late and were extremely unpopular.[468] High inflation became a pressing problem.

The Nixon administration needed to stop the increase in prices. Since Nixon considered inflation as the primary macroeconomic problem, as Rosenberg explains, the president set up an anti-inflation program, which included measures such as cutting federal expenditures, ending the investment tax credit, and extending the tax surcharge; furthermore, the FED implemented a very restrictive monetary policy.[469] This restrictive policy caused a mild recession, and unemployment rates rose from 3.5 to 4.9 percent between 1969 and 1970. The economy

---

[464] Johnson, *Vantage Point*, 439.

[465] Jeffry A. Frieden, *Global Capitalism: Its Fall and Rise in the Twentieth Century* (New York Norton, 2006), 344.

[466] Rosenberg, *American Economic Development*, 115–16.

[467] Johnson, *Vantage Point*, 439.

[468] Rosenberg, *American Economic Development*, 117–18; Gallup polls in January 1968 showed that 79 percent of the Americans rejected tax raises. See Johnson, *Vantage Point*, 440.

[469] Rosenberg, *American Economic Development*, 119.

reacted differently than the government had expected: inflation accelerated while workers pressed for higher wages, and unemployment increased—a stagflation crisis occurred.[470] Hence, the government needed to implement extreme measures, and in August 1970, the Economic Stabilization Act authorized the president to freeze "prices, rents, wages, interest rates, and salaries at levels not less than those prevailing on May 25, 1970."[471] Prices and wages were now under government control.

The United States additionally suffered from a balance of payments crisis. Frieden writes that the government artificially strengthened the dollar by keeping the exchange rates toward other currencies constant, which devaluated the dollar holdings of foreign countries because they could buy less with their dollars.[472] According to Rosenberg, the growing prices on the U.S. market made American products less competitive and foreign goods relatively cheaper, which turned the balance of payments deficit negative with tremendous effects since the surplus usually had been used to finance military commitments abroad.[473] Johnson claims that the inflationary erosion of the dollar, economic crises, and speculation made foreign countries such as the United Kingdom and France convert their dollar holdings into gold.[474] Between 1961 and 1968, as Frieden explains, more than 40 percent of the U.S. Gold reserves were taken up by cashing in dollars; the world lost confidence in the U.S. currency.[475] The run on U.S. gold needed to be stopped.

Nixon announced a new economic policy. On August 15, 1971, as Arthur Menzies Johnson writes, Nixon unleashed the full spectrum of economic interventions such as wage-price controls, to combat unem-

---

[470] Rosenberg, *American Economic Development*, 120.
[471] 116 Cong. Rec. S27,299 (daily ed. Aug. 4, 1970).
[472] Frieden, *Global Capitalism*, 344.
[473] Rosenberg, *American Economic Development*, 120.
[474] Johnson, *Vantage Point*, 316.
[475] Frieden, *Global Capitalism*, 345.

ployment and inflation, and suspension of the convertibility of the dollar into gold.[476] Rosenberg explains that the closing of the "gold window" required new international money arrangements, which necessitated a devaluation of the dollar. Domestic politics saw such the measure as a defeat, which encouraged Nixon to impose surcharges on imports and demand other countries to revalue upward their currencies.[477] West Germany, for instance, as Johnson explains, was such a candidate since it was in good economic shape and benefited from huge inflows of foreign exchange from the significant numbers of allied forces present there; the return flow to the United States was disproportionate.[478] Hence, West Germany became the subject of relentless attacks that demanded compensation for the balance of trade deficits.

According to Rosenberg, stagflation remained a severe macroeconomic problem during the 1970s. The problem even accelerated as a result of events such as the oil crisis in 1973; even the devaluation of the dollar, freed from fixed gold-dollar exchange rates with the dollar price being set by the international finance markets, did not stop the crisis.[479] In short, the effects of stagflation determined the debates about the American military commitments to Europe, and many U.S. senators believed that the West Germans should shoulder a greater burden of the defense of Europe.

c. East-West Relationship—From Détente to Yom Kippur

In the 1960s and 1970s, East-West hostility was in abeyance. Ian Q. R. Thomas explains that three factors paved the way to détente: strategic nuclear parity, the fragmentation of the Communist bloc, and the rise of a united and vocal Western Europe, exemplified by the West German *Ostpolitik*.[480] With the European members in the lead, NATO also

---

[476] Arthur Menzies Johnson, *The American Economy: An Historical Introduction to the Problems of the 1970's* (New York: Free Press, 1974), 66, 226.
[477] Rosenberg, *American Economic Development*, 120.
[478] Johnson, *Vantage Point*, 320.
[479] Rosenberg provides a compelling overview of the stagflation between 1971 and 1980. See Rosenberg, *American Economic Development*, 183–207.
[480] Thomas, *Promise of Alliance*, 88.

contributed to the détente process. For instance, in December 1967, according to Thomas, NATO adopted the Harmel Report, calling for military strength and solidarity but also emphasizing dialogue with the Soviets, which translated into the desire to explore arms control with the Warsaw Pact in the form of mutual and balanced force reductions (MBFR).[481] Thomas further writes that the Soviet invasion of Czechoslovakia in 1968 strained détente, but the reciprocal acceptance of MBFR in 1971 and plans for the Conference on Security and Cooperation in Europe eased the tensions.[482] Former Secretary of State Henry Kissinger explains that the Nixon administration was skeptical about détente, but such a position entailed the risk of becoming isolated in NATO and encouraged the European allies to adopt a reserved stance toward transatlantic security; détente needed substance instead of "atmospheric" talks.[483] That substantial contribution was the U.S.-Soviet Strategic Arms Limitation Talks (SALT) in 1969. Kissinger writes that the European allies stressed the importance of SALT but also feared the end of American nuclear superiority, which would leave the Soviets with considerable advantages in conventional forces.[484] The reduction of nuclear forces required a higher level of conventional troops, but the Europeans did not want to fill the gap, and critics—among them Mansfield—even came to the "amazing conclusion" that America should reduce its already inferior conventional presence in Europe.[485] Détente and its concomitants such as MBFR would later become a central argument in the troop reduction debates.

The Yom Kippur War strained the relationship between the United States and the Soviet Union. In October 1973, Egyptian and Syrian forces launched a surprise attack on Israel. As an immediate response, according to Thomas, the United States conducted a massive airlift to Israel, but some European NATO allies refused to grant overflight

---

[481] Thomas, *Promise of Alliance*, 90–91.

[482] Ibid., 92, 94.

[483] Henry, Kissinger, *White House Years* (Boston: Little, Brown and Company, 1979), 403.

[484] Ibid., 404.

[485] Ibid., 200.

rights since they feared an Arab oil embargo, which later came anyway.[486] Thomas further writes that the Soviets supported Egypt and Syria and threatened to intervene unilaterally if the United States would not cooperate in separating the belligerents, and as an answer to the Soviet threat, the Americans initiated a worldwide nuclear alert without consulting the NATO allies.[487] Although the crisis calmed down immediately and the belligerents accepted a ceasefire, the Yom Kippur War had negative effects on the U.S.-Soviet relationship, which in the late phases of the Mansfield debates would become an important counter-argument against U.S. troop reductions in Europe.

2. August 1966 to September 1970—Mansfield's Resolutions

The domestic economic situation was the main motive for Mansfield's proposals. Between 1966 and 1970, Mansfield introduced three resolutions that called for a substantial reduction of U.S. troops in Europe. Williams writes that Mansfield revolted against the president's excessive interpretation of the Tokin Gulf Resolution, and the senator believed that the European allies were free riding on U.S. security guarantees.[488] However, as James R. Golden explains, the senator never linked his proposals to specific political actions; his attempts, however, strengthened those who used the threat of force reductions as a tool for negotiations with the NATO allies.[489] Finally, the financial crisis fostered calls for a reduction of military spending, and Mansfield was not willing to sacrifice economy and welfare "on the altar of national security."[490] Thus, the conditions were set for an attack on the conduct of U.S. foreign military policy.

---

[486] Thomas, *Promise of Alliance*, 104.

[487] Ibid.

[488] Williams, *Senate and U.S. Troops in Europe*, 141–42.

[489] James R. Golden, *NATO Burden-sharing: Risks and Opportunities* (New York: Praeger, 1982), 55.

[490] Williams, *Senate and U.S. Troops in Europe*, 264.

The first resolution failed for various reasons. Mansfield introduced Senate Resolution 300 on August 31, 1966, calling for a substantial reduction of the U.S. troops in Europe.[491] In an address before the Carolina Forum of the University of North Carolina, Mansfield explained the rationale of his initiative:

> We have found ourselves plunged, hands, feet, and head into the mainstream of the world's affairs. We did not seek this role. We did not want it. Most of us still find the clothes of a great international power, costly, ill-fitting, and uncomfortable. Nevertheless, we are unable to get out of them. ... Our allies in Western Europe are much closer to the firing line; yet, in a period of unprecedented economic prosperity they are most unwilling to carry their pledged share. ... I have, therefore, joined with 43 other Senators in the introduction of a resolution, which recommends to the President that the Executive Branch make substantial reductions in the present deployment of our forces in Western Europe. Personally, I have felt for several years that two or three rather than six divisions would be more than sufficient to underscore our adherence to the North Atlantic Treaty. ... To talk of six divisions as a manifestation of international resolution and two divisions as an indication of a revived isolationism is to reveal how irrelevant if not downright misleading these terms have become.[492]

Although opponents had accused Mansfield of spurring isolationism, his real concern was fair burden sharing. Some senators, however, resisted Mansfield's plans since he had not provided the opportunity for exploring the initiative in formal hearings. As Williams reports, besides these procedural issues, the senators saw the initiative as an attack on

---

[491] An excerpt of the resolution is quoted in Johnson, *Vantage Point*, 307.

[492] Michael J. Mansfield, "Central Concerns of American Foreign Policy," Montana Memory Project, Montana State Library, March 13, 1967, 4, 9, 10, http://mtmemory.org/cdm/singleitem/collection/p16013coll41/id/1391/rec/726.

the president's executive supremacy in foreign affairs, and thus the Senate postponed the decision to January 1967.[493] In short, the Senate was not yet ready for a frontal attack on the president.

Talks between the allies reduced the urgency of the initiative. In October 1966, as James Edward Schwartz explains, trilateral negotiations between the United States, the United Kingdom, and West Germany about a balanced revision of force levels started; Mansfield suspended his plans, but when Great Britain announced a reduction of the Rhine Army in December 1966, the senator claimed that the trilateral talks were a waste of time.[494] On January 19, 1967, Mansfield reintroduced his resolution, signaling that the European allies could not indefinitely expect U.S. support.[495] In May 1967, as Williams explains, the U.S. State Department announced the withdrawal of 35,000 U.S. troops from Europe and a German $500 million purchase of U.S. bonds to compensate the balance of payments deficit.[496] Mansfield welcomed the agreement, and the Senate did not see the need to proceed with the resolution.[497] According to Schwartz, a few weeks later, Germany announced a reduction of its armed forces by up to 60,000 men within the next three years, which exasperated the senator, but he understood that further pressure in the immediate aftermath of the trilateral agreement was inappropriate, and thus he suspended his efforts.[498] The marginal troop reduction had defused the situation but not permanently solved the problem.

In 1968, a confluence of factors thwarted Mansfield's plans. According to Rosenberg, inflation had accelerated in 1967, which forced the Johnson administration to cut nondefense expenditures and introduce

---

[493] Williams, *Senate and U.S. Troops in Europe*, 146–48.

[494] James Edmond Schwartz, "Senator Michael J. Mansfield and United States Military Disengagement from Europe: A Case Study in American Foreign Policy: The Majority Leader, His Amendment, and His Influence upon the Senate" (PhD diss., University of North Carolina, 1977), 80.

[495] 113 Cong. Rec. S967 (daily ed. Jan. 19, 1967) (statement of Sen. Clark).

[496] Williams, *Senate and U.S. Troops in Europe*, 152–53; for further details, see Johnson, *Vantage Point, 306–11*.

[497] Williams, *Senate and U.S. Troops in Europe*, 153.

[498] Schwartz, "United States Military Disengagement from Europe," 86.

a 10 percent income tax surcharge.[499] Deficits reached tremendous heights, which put the dollar under severe pressure, as Williams writes.[500] When the Vietnam War required the extension of the draft, Senator Stuart Symington called for a shift of well-trained U.S. troops from Europe to South East Asia instead of sending hastily trained draftees to Vietnam. Thus, he introduced an amendment to the Defense Procurement Bill (S3293) on April 19, 1968, which prohibited the financing of more than 50,000 troops in Europe after December 31, 1968.[501] According to Schwartz, Symington was convinced—as Mansfield was—that one division in Europe was a sufficient conventional contribution to European defense. A war with the Soviet Union would immediately go nuclear; thus, a large number of U.S. troops would make no difference, and the European allies would never increase their efforts if the United States maintained the high level of troops in Europe.[502] Surprisingly, Symington withdrew his amendment since it seemed more promising to attach it to the Military Appropriation Bill (HR 18707) later that year.[503] On August 20, 1968, according to Williams, the Soviet invasion of Czechoslovakia derailed Symington's plans because congressional support receded dramatically.[504] The plans had to wait until the next congressional season.

NATO reacted cautiously to troop reduction plans. According to L. James Binder, SACEUR General Lyman Lemnitzer opposed any cuts during congressional hearings and conceded that draining the U.S. presence in Europe due to the Vietnam War would seriously impair the allied mission.[505] On April 2, 1968, Congresswoman Edna F. Kelly announced that Lemnitzer had not convinced her because the NATO allies had not responded to the increased Soviet threat yet. Now, due

---

[499] Rosenberg, *American Economic Development*, 117–18.

[500] Williams, *Senate and U.S. Troops in Europe*, 155.

[501] 114 Cong. Rec. S10,035 (daily ed. Apr. 19, 1968).

[502] Schwartz, "United States Military Disengagement from Europe," 88–89.

[503] 114 Cong. Rec. S10,035 (daily ed. Apr. 19, 1968) (statement of Sen. Symington).

[504] Williams, *Senate and U.S. Troops in Europe*, 158.

[505] L. James Binder, *Lemnitzer: A Soldier for His Time* (Washington, DC: Brassey's, 1997), 323–24.

to domestic demands, the United States would have to reduce the number of conventional troops in Western Europe because America could not shoulder the burden any more.[506] Despite congressional resistance, in early 1969, as Sean Kay writes, President-elect Richard Nixon reassured NATO Secretary General Manlio Brosio that troop reductions would only be conducted in the context of MBFR and not unilaterally.[507] As a result, the final communiqué of the NATO Defense Planning Committee meeting on May 28, 1969, reads, "[The current NATO strategy requires] the presence of substantial ... North American and European conventional forces. ... The overall military capability of NATO should not be reduced except as part of a pattern of mutual force reductions balanced in scope and timing."[508] In other words, the NATO allies had not yet done enough to address U.S. concerns, but Nixon reassured NATO that the United States would not conduct unilateral reductions before consulting with the allies.

Despite these arrangements, Nixon wanted to raise the pressure on the European allies, and Mansfield's attempts played into his hand. For instance, in 1969, Schwartz writes, the United States and Germany agreed on a two-year offset agreement worth $1.52 billion; in return, the Americans promised not to alter the U.S. troop presence in Europe.[509] This deal offended Mansfield, so he reintroduced his proposal on December 1, 1969, which marked a fundamental attack on Nixon's foreign and domestic policies. In the eyes of the senator, the "Europeanization of the defense in Europe" made no progress at a time when the United States was short on resources.[510] Obviously, the government was not willing to make fundamental changes in the conduct of foreign policy.

---

[506] 114 Cong. Rec. H8,594 (daily ed. Apr. 2, 1968) (statement of Rep. Kelly).
[507] Sean Kay, *NATO and the Future of European Security* (Lanham, MD: Rowman & Littlefield, 1998), 49.
[508] "Final Communiqué," North Atlantic Treaty Organization, May, 28, 1969, http://www.nato.int/cps/en/natohq/official_texts_26765.htm?selectedLocale=en.
[509] Schwartz, "United States Military Disengagement from Europe," 101–3.
[510] Williams, *Senate and U.S. Troops in Europe*, 162–63.

The administration even sought an open confrontation with Mansfield. For instance, on January 20, 1970, Undersecretary of State Elliot Richardson gave a forceful speech before the Chicago Council on World Affairs, arguing against Mansfield's troop reduction plans and putting the senator in the defensive.[511] Reciprocally, Mansfield resubmitted his resolution on January 21, 1970.[512] The president's answer then was the Nixon Doctrine, which announced that each ally nation was in charge of its own security; on February 18, 1970, he said, "The United States will participate in the defense and development of allies and friends, but ... America cannot—and will not— ... undertake all the defense of the free nations of the world. We will help where it makes a real difference and is considered in our interest."[513] In sum, the tenacity of Mansfield's pressure gave the Nixon doctrine a great urgency.

The combined approach of Mansfield and Nixon alarmed the NATO allies. In 1969, Thomas writes, some European NATO members had formed the EUROGROUP to coordinate their defense efforts but had achieved very little since then.[514] In September 1970, Kissinger explains, Nixon gave the project a new impetus by announcing that the United States would prefer additional military contributions to European defense instead of subsidies for the stationing of troops; American soldiers should not "act as mercenaries for Europeans."[515] The European answer, according to Williams, was the European Defense Improvement Program, which envisaged spending about $1 billion in the following five years in exchange for the assurance that the United States would maintain the status quo of troop levels in Europe; and the president agreed.[516] Clearly, Nixon and Mansfield were on a

---

[511] 116 Cong. Rec. S921-3 (daily ed. Jan. 23, 1970).

[512] 116 Cong. Rec. S511 (daily ed. Jan. 21, 1970) (statement Sen. Mansfield).

[513] Richard Nixon, "U.S. Foreign policy for the 1970s: A New Strategy for Peace," Office of the Historian, Bureau of Public Affairs, United States Department of State, February 18, 1970, https://history.state.gov/historicaldocuments/frus1969-76v01/d60.

[514] Thomas, *Promise of Alliance*, 102.

[515] Kissinger, *White House Years*, 400.

[516] Williams, *Senate and U.S. Troops in Europe*, 166.

collision course. To stop these trade-offs, the senator had to bring out the heavy artillery.

3. May 1971 to November 1971—Mansfield's Strategy Change

Mansfield changed his strategy, but Nixon fought back. On May 11, 1971, the senator introduced an amendment to the Selective Service Bill (HR 6531), which demanded a 50 percent reduction of U.S. troops in Europe until the end of the year.[517] Williams explains that the previous resolutions had no binding character; the Selective Service Bill, however, was a law that Nixon could only veto as a whole. On the other hand, the president needed the draft extension to sustain the Vietnam War.[518] Kissinger asserts that the administration was determined to defeat the amendment but faced severe obstacles since the proposal coincided with the final negotiations on SALT and the future of Berlin, and Mansfield was jeopardizing these attempts. Furthermore, any compromise would open the "floodgates" for further troop reductions.[519] Thus, the president needed to defeat the amendment using all means.

Nixon activated former officials to lobby against Mansfield's proposal. On May 13, 1971, as Kissinger reports, the president met high-ranking former officials, among them Secretary of State Dean Acheson; former High Commissioners of Germany John J. McCloy and Lucius D. Clay; former Ambassador to the UN Henry Cabot Lodge; and former Supreme Allied Commanders Europe Alfred M. Gruenther, Lauris Norstad, and Lemnitzer.[520] Nixon asked the Atlanticists for their support in lobbying against Mansfield; the "Old Guard" agreed and unleashed an extensive campaign.[521] Additionally, unexpected support

---

[517] 117 Cong. Rec. S14,401 (daily ed. May 11, 1971).

[518] Williams, *Senate and U.S. Troops in Europe*, 169.

[519] Kissinger, *White House Years*, 940–41.

[520] Ibid., 944.

[521] Details about the campaign are described in Ibid., 944-7; Williams, *Senate and U.S. Troops in Europe*, 174–92; Schwartz, "United States Military Disengagement from Europe," 118–22.

came from the Soviet side. Schwartz writes that on May 14, 1971, General Secretary Leonid Ilyich Brezhnev announced the Warsaw Pact's readiness to begin negotiations over mutual troop reductions in Europe.[522] The timing could not have been more unfortunate for Mansfield. On May 19, 1971, the senator held an impassioned speech. He said,

> I am not a member of the old guard. ... Their voices have been revitalized today, Mr. President. But the world they address is quite different. Europe's economic and social recovery has been remarkable. ... It all adds up to this Nation carrying a very one-sided financial burden for NATO. ... Let the European pocketbook determine how critically the Europeans view the presence of 300,000 servicemen. ... Time and time again we have admonished our allies to bear a fair share of the NATO burden. ... We have already paid too big price for delaying this question with negotiations and consultations.[523]

Thus, the majority leader did not seek to end the U.S. involvement in NATO; instead, he wanted to bring the financial burden closer into line with that of other members. He also warned the administration not to intertwine the deteriorating security situation in the Middle East with the calls for troop reductions in Europe—a herald of the 1973 debate.[524] Finally, the vote on his proposal went down by 61 to 36.[525] Nixon's lobbying had been successful.

NATO was less optimistic and prepared for the worst. C. Richard Nelson writes that Nixon had sent the new SACEUR General Andrew J. Goodpaster to convince Mansfield to stop his attempts since the U.S. troop contribution was vital for NATO—a fact the senator did not

---

[522] Schwartz, "United States Military Disengagement from Europe," 116.
[523] 117 Cong. Rec. S15,948 (daily ed. May 19, 1971) (statement Sen. Mansfield).
[524] Ibid., S15,945.
[525] Ibid., S15,960.

disclaim; however, Goodpaster could not change Mansfield's mind.[526] Nelson further explains that Goodpaster even ordered his staff to develop plans on how to best compensate for sudden reductions of NATO forces.[527] NATO obviously understood the urgency of the situation.

Nixon's financial policy encouraged Mansfield to launch a new proposal. On August 15, 1971, Arthur M. Johnson writes, the president introduced the full spectrum of drastic stabilization measures such as wage-price controls and increased import taxes; furthermore, he suspended the convertibility of the dollar into gold and devaluated the dollar.[528] Thus, the U.S. economy was in serious trouble. On September 14, 1971, Mansfield spoke before the Senate on "The New Economic Program and Western Europe," arguing that détente made a large U.S. troop presence in Europe obsolete, and a significant reduction would be "in accord with the Nation's domestic and international economic interests."[529] Finally, on November 17, 1971, the Senate Appropriations Committee voted to attach an amendment to the Defense Appropriations Bill (HR 11731) that prohibited the funding of more than 250,000 troops in Europe after June 15, 1972—a moderate reduction of 50,000 troops.[530] Williams reports that the president sent a letter to the Senate, which stressed the importance of SALT, the Berlin negotiations, and the MBFR talks by NATO Secretary Brosio in the following week. Mansfield's proposal was troubleshooting these initiatives.[531] Because of Nixon's intervention, Mansfield received a 54 to 39 negative vote.[532] Compared to the vote in May 1971, the senator, however, had found more supporters.

---

[526] C. Richard Nelson, *The Life and Work of General Andrew J. Goodpaster: Best Practices in National Security Affairs* (Lanham, MD: Rowman & Littlefield, 2016), 219.
[527] Ibid.
[528] Johnson, *American Economy*, 66, 226.
[529] 117 Cong. Rec. S31,693 (daily ed. Sep. 14, 1971) (statement Sen. Mansfield).
[530] See Williams, *Senate and U.S. Troops in Europe*, 201.
[531] Ibid., 202.
[532] Ibid., 202–3.

4. April 1973 to September 1973—Peak of Pressure

The year 1973 marked the peak of the troop reduction debate. On April 23, 1973, Kissinger heralded the Year of Europe and explained that a flexible response needed a credible conventional defense.[533] He claimed, "The United Sates has global interests and responsibilities. Our European allies have regional interests."[534] Thus, the roles within the alliance were clear and everybody knew how the United States interpreted the transatlantic partnership. Furthermore, Kissinger asserted that the strategy of flexible response needed a credible conventional defense, and since the United States owed its people a defense posture "at the safest minimum size and cost," the allies would need to share more of the burden of European defense.[535]

Kissinger's words were grist for the mill of those demanding troop reductions in Europe. Williams explains that financial deficits made the troops abroad a luxury that many Americans did not want to pay for, especially since Nixon cut funds for hospital building and urban renewal but left the defense budget untouched.[536] Critics, for instance, described Nixon's policy as "nothing less than the systematic dismantling and destruction of the greatest social programs and the great precedents of humanitarian government inaugurated by Franklin D. Roosevelt and enlarged by every Democratic President since then."[537] In the international field, some senators were also skeptical about the progress of the MBFR talks, which in their eyes undermined congressional attempts to withdraw troops unilaterally.[538] Furthermore, the senators were convinced that a limited U.S. presence was sufficient to act as a

---

[533] Henry Kissinger, "8. Address by the President's Assistant for National Security Affairs," Office of the Historian, Bureau of Public Affairs, United States Department of State, April 23, 1973, https://history.state.gov/historicaldocuments/frus1969-76v38p1/d8.

[534] Ibid.

[535] Ibid.

[536] Williams, *Senate and U.S. Troops in Europe*, 210.

[537] Ibid., 211.

[538] Phil Williams, "What Happened to the Mansfield Amendment?" *Survival* 18, no. 4 (1976): 148, doi:10.1080/00396337608441623.

tripwire for U.S. nuclear guarantees.[539] Finally, Nixon's Imperial Presidency and the Watergate scandal, after 1973, encouraged Congress to challenge Nixon whenever possible.[540] The field was prepared for a new resolution.

New legislation called for worldwide troop reductions. Since Mansfield's opponents had proven to withstand all initiatives against the withdrawal of forces from Europe, the senator had to change his strategy. Instead of focusing on Europe, Mansfield now proposed a global reduction by 50 percent, which the Democratic Policy Committee further raised to 66 percent, Williams writes.[541] In March 1973, however, the Senate Democratic caucus defanged the proposal and called for a "substantial reduction" by mid-1974.[542] The administration's argumentation echoed previous debates but placed greater emphasis on financial aspects since most of Mansfield's supporters resented the costs of the troops abroad.[543] For instance, Secretary of Defense James Rodney Schlesinger said, "Most of the deployed forces are supplied by our allies—something on the order of 90 per cent of the ground forces, 80 per cent of the ships, and 75 per cent of the aircraft."[544] Thus, the administration addressed the senators' concerns, which relieved the pressure from the debate.

Mansfield was not alone in his fight. On September 24, 1973, Mansfield raised the question, "Why should we, 3,000 miles away, assume such arrogance as to perceive a greater threat to Europe than the Europeans?"[545] The only logical consequence for the United States would be to acknowledge détente, realize economic realities, fulfill the demands of the American people, and withdraw the troops.[546] On September 25, 1973, Senators Henry Jackson and Sam Nunn introduced

---

[539] Williams, "What Happened to the Mansfield Amendment?" 148.
[540] Ibid.
[541] Williams, *Senate and U.S. Troops in Europe*, 211.
[542] Ibid., 212.
[543] Williams, *Senate and U.S. Troops in Europe*, 218.
[544] Quoted in Ibid.
[545] 119 Cong. Rec. S31,155 (daily ed. Sep. 24, 1973) (statement Sen. Mansfield).
[546] Ibid., S31,156.

an amendment to the Defense Procurement Bill that demanded a reduction of American troops abroad equal to the percentage of the balance of payments shortfall.[547] Williams writes that Nixon did not oppose the proposal since it deprived Mansfield of his financial arguments. Consequently, the amendment passed with an overwhelming majority of 84 to 5.[548] Unabashed, Mansfield introduced an additional proposal, which asked for a worldwide troop reduction by 50 percent over the next three years.[549] Prior to the vote, Mansfield modified his demands to 40 percent, and—to the surprise of many—it passed by 49 to 46.[550] According to Williams, the proposal would replace an earlier amendment by Senator Alan Cranston of California; thus, a second vote was necessary to attach the measure to the defense procurement bill, and the Senate scheduled the vote for the afternoon, which offered the possibility for intensive lobbying.[551] During the second vote, the Senate rejected the amendment in a 51 to 44 split.[552] Thus, a technicality had prevented Mansfield's success. On the following day, according to Williams, Senators Humphrey and Cranston introduced an amendment that called for a 23 percent reduction by the end of 1975, and although the administration battled over this initiative, too, it passed with a 48 to 36 vote since many senators felt that Mansfield had been humiliated the day before.[553] Troop reduction became law. Fortunately, the Yom Kippur War solved Nixon's dilemma, undermined the Senate's position, and made the troop withdrawal obsolete.

5. June 1974 to June 1975—Final Defeat

In 1974 and 1975, the congressional pressure for troop reductions declined. According to Williams, in response to the Yom Kippur War, the

---

[547] 119 Cong. Rec. S31,311 (daily ed. Sep. 25, 1973).
[548] Williams, *Senate and U.S. Troops in Europe*, 220.
[549] 119 Cong. Rec. S31,510 (daily ed. Sep. 26, 1973).
[550] Ibid., S31,521–22.
[551] Williams, *Senate and U.S. Troops in Europe*, 221.
[552] 119 Cong. Rec. S31,569 (daily ed. Sep. 26, 1973).
[553] Williams, *Senate and U.S. Troops in Europe*, 224–25.

Senate no longer accepted détente as an argument to substitute for deterrence. Even so, the MBFR talks had officially started on October 30, 1973.[554] Williams further explains that the failure to consult with the NATO allies over the nuclear alert on October 25, 1973, strained U.S. relations with the Europeans, who also had severe economic problems because of the energy crisis.[555] On the other hand, the United States substantially improved its balance of payments deficit and the Jackson-Nunn initiative was making progress.[556] Under these circumstances, Mansfield's timing was unfortunate because his economic arguments faded away.

Mansfield also received stiff opposition from within the Senate. According to Williams, Nunn wanted to avoid an immediate nuclear conflict by maintaining a conventional forces threshold. Thus, he recommended an improvement in the U.S. military tooth-to-tail ratio in Europe by a moderate reduction of only 23,000 support troops—later reduced to 18,000.[557] Nunn had the support of Schlesinger, which made his initiative more attractive than Mansfield's meat axe approach. Nevertheless, Mansfield introduced another amendment on June 6, 1974, which called for a worldwide reduction and demobilization of 125,000 troops by the end of 1975.[558] This reduction would have made a diminution of the European presence unavoidable. Williams reports that Nunn was Mansfield's strongest critic; finally, the Senate rejected Mansfield's proposal by 54 to 35.[559] With Nunn, the opposition was much more sophisticated than ever before. Thus, Mansfield had to postpone his plans to the following year once again.

As the Vietnam War finally ended, the support for Mansfield's proposals declined dramatically. In 1974, as Williams writes, the Jackson-Nunn initiative had fully covered the balance of payments deficit, and

---

[554] Williams, "What Happened to the Mansfield Amendment?" 149.
[555] Ibid.
[556] Ibid., 150.
[557] Williams, *Senate and U.S. Troops in Europe*, 244–45.
[558] 120 Cong. Rec. S18,009 (daily ed. Jun. 6, 1974).
[559] Williams, *Senate and U.S. Troops in Europe*, 249.

NATO members had increased their defense efforts.[560] MBFR talks had not made much progress, and the overall security situation on Europe's southern periphery was in disarray. For instance, in 1974, the Greek-Turkish conflict over Cyprus erupted, Portugal was in severe political turmoil, and the Vietnam War debacle ended with the fall of Saigon in 1975.[561] Due to the overall situation, Mansfield abstained from introducing another amendment. During a Senate debate on U.S. foreign policy in June 1975, his strongest supporter Senator Cranston said, "It would be unwise at this particular time to make any reductions because it might give others the mistaken impression that we are on the run and turning inward and becoming isolationist."[562] In times of international turmoil, a troop reduction would send the wrong signal to America's allies and adversaries. Consequently, as Williams explains, the Senate did not even bring to a roll call Senator Mike Gravel's amendment, which demanded a reduction of 200,000 troops abroad.[563] Mansfield's continuous proposals for U.S. troop reductions in Europe came to a bitter end. With his retirement in 1976, the subject disappeared from the political agenda. The potential for controversy, however, remained.

---

[560] Williams, *Senate and U.S. Troops in Europe*, 254.
[561] Ibid.
[562] Quoted in Ibid., 255.
[563] Ibid., 256.

IV. CONCLUSION

The starting point of this book was U.S. President Trump's 2016 election campaign rhetoric regarding NATO, which encouraged critics to describe his envisaged policy as isolationist. In April 2017, after a few months in office, President Trump adjusted much of this strong rhetoric, but a few key elements of his strategy remain.

This work should enhance the reader's understanding of the United States' reluctance to adopt an internationalist foreign policy. This reluctance is deeply rooted, yet when confronted with the result of the 2016 election, many NATO allies seemed surprised by this stance. Thus, this work analyzed the origins of isolationism in the American experience of statecraft. In this context, the three main hypotheses were: (a) isolationism is deeply rooted in the country's historical traditions; (b) foreign policy *vis-à-vis* Europe (and NATO) is shaped, to a high degree, by domestic politics; (c) America has an implied leadership role in the Western hemisphere as a promoter of security and democratic values due to its economic and military predominance. Based on the analyses of the case studies, the aim of the work was to assess the possible implications of past foreign policy decisions on U.S. security commitments to Europe and NATO in the near term.

This chapter covers two areas. First, it provides a short summary of the findings of the case studies in relation to the previously mentioned hypotheses. Second, it extracts certain themes of Trump's foreign policy, as far as they are already clear, and compares these themes to those represented in the case studies to discern America's likely conduct of foreign policy and security commitments to Europe under the new administration.

A. Testing the Hypotheses

The first of the following subsections covers the hypothesis that isolationism is deeply rooted in the history of U.S. foreign policy. Given that this work is unapologetically historical and that isolationist notions have been recurrent themes in all four cases, the analysis of the case studies confirmed the first hypothesis. However, isolationism manifested itself in slightly different ways. Hence, the question is whether such a conduct of statecraft is exceptional in any case and whether certain facets of isolationist foreign policy remain consistent in practice. The second hypothesis focused on the influence of the domestic political situation in pursuing foreign policy. With a special emphasis on Hanhimäki's criteria, the second subsection analyzes how factors such as economy, ethnicity, election cycles, party politics, and morality affected the conduct of U.S. foreign policy. The last subsection examines how America's economic and military strength in combination with its self-imposed leadership role contributes to the U.S. role as a promoter of peace and security in Europe. Motives to intervene militarily might have been different in each of the periods studied, but an interventionist policy has most often best served U.S. interests.

1. Variations of Isolationism in the Historic Context

U.S. isolationist tradition follows the ideas of President Washington's 1769 Farewell Address and the 1823 Monroe Doctrine. Since the United States loathed getting involved in the political quarrels of the old continent, the country preferred a policy of non-entanglement from European affairs and avoided any alliances and stronger ties with Europe. Furthermore, the United States adhered to the idea that it executes control within a certain sphere of influence.

The First World War challenged the customs of non-entanglement in European affairs. Due to trade relations with the belligerent parties and diverging public interests, the United States adhered to the tradition of neutrality and non-involvement. Isolationism primarily meant not to intervene militarily in the European conflict, but to execute trade with the belligerent parties for the sake of the country's economic advancement. Thereby, the Americans followed President Washington's words, "The great rule of conduct for us in regard to foreign nations is in extending our commercial relations, to have with them as little political connection as possible."[564] For the United States, the sphere of interest, as far as it concerns national security, did not include the European continent yet. In 1823, President James Monroe announced that the United States would "consider any attempt on their part [the Europeans] to extend their system to any portion of this hemisphere as dangerous to our peace and safety."[565] With Germany's unrestricted U-boat war, U.S. economic interests were at stake; neutrality in military terms reached a dead end, and the United States had to go to war. President Wilson's vision of a new world order, with a League of Nations under U.S. leadership as a guardian for world peace, unnecessarily extended the U.S. sphere of interest, and thus, this plan did not endure much beyond 1920.

Given the lessons of the First World War, in the interwar period the idea of non-entanglement was exercised to the extreme. In the 1920s, amid a messy European peace settlement, the United States heavily involved itself in the reconstruction of Europe because economic expansionism needed stable markets and peace. Furthermore, the United States believed in the idea of being able to outlaw war by international agreements (Kellogg-Briand Pact). Once again, the United States followed Washington's words, "Harmony, liberal intercourse with all nations, are recommended by policy. … Our commercial policy should … give trade a stable course."[566] Military intervention was not an option, and the Americans withdrew their troops from Germany as quickly as possible.

With the growing tensions in Europe and confronted with the imminent risk of being drawn into new European conflicts during the 1930s, the Congress forced FDR's administration into inactivity by strict neutrality laws, which banned trading with belligerents. Thereby,

---

[564] George Washington, "Farewell Address," 100 Milestone Documents, U.S. National Archives and Records Administration, September 19, 1796, https://www.ourdocuments.gov/doc.php?doc=15&page=transcript.

[565] James Monroe, "Annual Message to Congress," 100 Milestone Documents, U.S. National Archives and Records Administration, December 2, 1823, https://www.ourdocuments.gov/doc.php?flash=true&doc=23&page=transcript.

[566] Washington, "Farewell Address."

the United States disentangled itself from world politics. Nevertheless, as soon as this legislation adversely affected the U.S. economy and as tensions grew in Europe, the Americans abstained from a too strict interpretation of this self-imposed economic neutrality. With the outbreak of the Second World War, the United States still believed that Britain and France could contain Germany, but Germany's quick wins in 1940 and new technologies, able to project air power over great distances, increased the fear of vulnerability. For the first time in history, the country's remote geographic position did not provide protection. Now, using Washington's words, "The detached and distant situation" no longer enabled the United States "to pursue a different course."[567] All of a sudden, Western Europe was in midst of the U.S. sphere of interest, and the United States had to intervene militarily.

The end of the Second World War confronted the United States with the question of whether to leave the security of the European continent in the hands of the Western allies. Economic prosperity as the source for political stability and security was the rule of the day, and the United States—once again, as the Farewell Address emphasized—focused on trade relations and U.S. economic expansionism. The economic and military weakness of the Western European powers, however, created a security vacuum that the Soviets were willing to fill. The United States, though, was not willing to tolerate the rise of a continental superpower, which would endanger U.S. predominance in the Western hemisphere. Europe was now part of the U.S. sphere of interest, which required a reinterpretation of the Monroe Doctrine.

To contain the Soviet threat, the United States abandoned the non-alliance provisions of the Farewell Address and established a close security partnership exemplified by NATO. Despite strong congressional resistance to any form of military intervention in Europe, troop commitments followed the political guarantees of the North Atlantic Pact, which then brought the issue of burden sharing to the forefront. During the debates in the 1960s and 1970s, the Senate did not question security guarantees for Europe per se. Given domestic problems such

---

[567] Washington, "Farewell Address."

as galloping inflation, unemployment, and the war in Vietnam, the Senate, however, challenged the scope of U.S. conventional commitments and, once again, brought the issue of fair burden sharing to the forefront.

In sum, the United States has an aversion to any form of binding commitments and alliances; however, the Americans are willing to deviate from this position when national interests such as commerce or security are at stake. With the Cold War, the sphere of interest extended to Western Europe. In fact, as Kissinger had pointed out in 1973, the United States had a worldwide focus. In times of domestic turmoil, especially during economic crises, the United States tends to turn inward and put a stronger emphasis on its isolationist traditions. As the cases showed, the spectrum of isolationist behavior hereby ranged from military non-intervention to full-fledged economic and military neutrality.

2. Influence of Domestic Policy

President Wilson based his foreign policy on his strong Kantian belief and was even willing to subordinate material interests to his moral principles. Nevertheless, his attempts as a mediator to preserve peace in Europe could not prevent the outbreak of the First World War. European immigrants significantly influenced the political course, and the fear of uprisings encouraged Wilson to take a neutral position toward the European belligerents, which did not mean non-involvement in all fields. Since the country was still recovering from an economic downturn, the Americans did not shy away from trading war material even if it included the risk of being plunged into the European conflict. During the 1916 election campaign, Wilson presented himself as the only choice to prevent war, and he ultimately defeated his Republican opponent Hughes who took a pro-war stand. The public honored the president's anti-war stand.

Wilson, however, falsely interpreted his victory as a confirmation of his internationalist policy, which put him at odds with his people. As Wilson envisaged it, the primary cause for entering the war in 1917 became the freedom of commerce, which Wilson disguised with a more compelling missionary objective of making the world safe against the German submarines. The president further molded his Kantian world view into a peace program and turned the 1918 mid-term congressional elections into a vote for confidence for his internationalist policy, which resulted in a loss of bipartisan support in foreign political affairs and backfired when Congress did not support his plans for the League of Nations. The ambitious president underestimated the country's strong reluctance to adopt an interventionist policy.

The rejection of the League covenant led to a new humility in foreign political affairs, and focused more attention on economic progress and commerce instead of world leadership. U.S. commercial expansionism worked best in a peaceful and stable environment, which the United States tried to create through the 1928 Kellogg-Briand Pact that caused a false sense of security among the U.S. public. In the 1930s, the Great Depression struck the United States, and the downturn consumed much of the president's attention. Furthermore, FDR made broad concessions to the isolationist right wing of his party to gain support as a presidential candidate. Since foreign policy now had a low priority, the U.S. public became convinced that the nation's involvement in the First World War was a fatal error. This belief nurtured anti-war interest groups that established strong influence on U.S. foreign policy, exemplified by the 1934 Nye investigation, which blamed bankers and munition makers for the U.S. entry into the First World War. The findings of the Nye Commission led to a series of neutrality laws limiting the president's agency in foreign politics. The worsening security situation in Europe and the economic effects of full-fledged abstinence from trade led to an adaptation of the neutrality laws.

Between 1940 and 1941, pressure groups such as the CDA and the America First Committee played a vital role in shaping public opinion. During the 1940 presidential election campaign, FDR did not confront true opposition concerning his foreign policy. Trade-offs with Republican candidate Willkie as well as clever moves that outmaneuvered his opponent enabled Roosevelt to keep the war issue out of the campaign. The 1940 bases-destroyer deal stretched his relationship with Congress to the extreme, but FDR had wide public support for his move, which presumably prevented a congressional revolt. In March 1941, opposition to the Lend-Lease Act was almost the last uprising of the isolationists. By September 1941, the United States was in an undeclared war with Germany over the freedom of the seas—as had happened in

1917. The lifting of the neutrality act in November 1941 concluded the slow move toward a more internationalist position, and the attack on Pearl Harbor in December 1941 removed all remaining obstacles.

The end of the Second World War in September 1945 presented the United States with severe domestic political challenges since the country had to transition from wartime to peacetime economy. Thus, President Truman's number-one priority became the solution of his domestic problems. His programs, though, confronted strong resistance from Congress, which led to substantial gains for the Republicans in the 1946 mid-term congressional election. Henceforth, the president received strong opposition also for his foreign policy. Meanwhile, the emergence of the Cold War increased the tension in foreign affairs, and the European powers demanded greater U.S. involvement in European security. Following its historic tradition, the United States primarily focused on trade and economic aid, but Europe needed substantial security guarantees—a transatlantic alliance.

In 1948, negotiations about the North Atlantic Treaty brought isolationist sentiments, partisan rivalries, and competence issues between the legislative and executive branches to the forefront. The Congress was not willing to agree to any form of war automatism, according to the initial provisions of Article V of the North Atlantic Pact. Furthermore, pledges for military aid, following Article III, raised the fear that the European allies would financially drain the United States—an issue hard to explain to U.S. voters. Only with substantial concessions did Congress implement the North Atlantic Treaty. Disillusionment came with Truman's proposal for a costly military assistance program. Meanwhile, NSC-68 called for a massive increase in defense spending, which nearly destroyed congressional willingness to make any financial concessions to the Europeans. In June 1950, the invasion of South Korea raised the fear of domino effects, which encouraged Truman to announce an increased troop presence in Europe in December 1950. Given the results of the congressional election in November 1950, the illness of Senator Vandenberg, and the growing influence of isolationist Senator Taft, Truman's announcement led to a broad debate in Congress, which lasted until April 1951. Nevertheless, a Senate resolution finally approved Truman's policy, urged the European NATO allies to take a fair burden in European defense, and demanded congressional approval for any future stationing of U.S. troops in Europe.

Almost two decades later, congressional attempts to enforce U.S. troop reductions in Europe exemplified partisan politics in the light of a domestic economic crisis. From the mid-1960s to the mid-1970s, the United States confronted the Vietnam War, a severe stagflation crisis with high inflation and unemployment, and a significant balance of payments deficit. Senator Mansfield and his fellow campaigners introduced several resolutions and amendments to reduce the number of U.S. troops in Europe since the senators believed that the NATO allies would not pay their fair share in the defense of Europe. Additionally, the senators were on a crusade against presidential authority in foreign political affairs, similar to the Great Debate in 1951. The debates during the Mansfield era, however, were mostly an issue of partisanship and personal animosities among Atlanticists, non-interventionists, and the administration; security guarantees to Europe per se were never seriously questioned. Unintentionally, Senate proposals even played into the hands of the executive branch because they increased the pressure on the European allies to strengthen their financial commitments to NATO. Since both administrations under Presidents Johnson and Nixon supported the transatlantic partnership, they had to prevent any concrete, far-reaching Senate legislation but preserve a certain amount of pressure on Europe.

In short, one could narrow down the influence of domestic politics on foreign political affairs to the famous quip "All politics is local." Furthermore, factors such as economy, interest groups, partisan politics, and individual beliefs and preferences of presidents, advisors, or other political figures had a strong influence on the country's foreign political course. In this context, one could repeat Kennan's verdict about the making of U.S. foreign policy, in which public opinion easily leads Washington officials astray into emotionalism and subjectivity. Finally, however, political realities dictated the U.S. course in the international realm.

3. U.S. Leadership Role

President Wilson saw the United States as the leader of a new world order, but the U.S. public was not yet ready for such a radical change. Wilson, however, was misled by the false belief that he would be able to educate the U.S. people to accept these new responsibilities of world leadership. Wilson's plans for the League of Nations backfired and the country returned to a position of strict neutrality after the First World War. Yet, America sought peace and stability through disentanglement from European affairs. With the end of the First World War, however, the United States had become an economic and military superpower. Thus, disentanglement from world affairs was not a realistic option any more.

FDR understood the new role of the United States and initiated a change of U.S. foreign policy by emphasizing the interdependence of world politics and the impracticability of isolationism. In the president's view, the United States had to restore world order, fight the lawlessness in the international system, and actively engage itself in the quest for peace. Hence, for the United States it was a moral obligation to support the Western powers in the fight against Nazi Germany and prevent the rise of a continental superpower able to challenge U.S. security and economic predominance.

The United States emerged from the Second World War as an unprecedented economic and military superpower whereas the former great powers of Europe had disintegrated in the wake of war. Although the Americans were highly reluctant to adopt a leadership role, the spread of communism and the gentle pressure of the European allies finally made the United States the leader of NATO. America saw it as an obligation to prevent the Sovietization of Western Europe similar to the U.S. entry into war in 1941, which hindered Nazi Germany from becoming a continental superpower.

Cold War security guarantees to the European allies meant also the stationing of U.S. troops in Europe, and a new internationalism replaced isolationist traditions. The U.S. troop presence in Europe, however, included the risk of being bound indefinitely to European security affairs. Hence, debates about burden sharing dominated the disputes between the United States and its NATO allies in the following decades. Thereby, the threat of reducing its commitments to Europe and refraining from the leadership role became a bargaining chip for the United States to press the European partners to pay their fair share in the defense of Europe. Nevertheless, the United States never seriously questioned its leadership role in NATO although domestic political realities occasionally pushed manifest destiny aside.

In sum, since the end of the First World War, the United States has become such an important economic and military power that it could not easily disentangle itself from world politics. Most important, U.S. predominance in security affairs and the economic field is a result of its interventionist policy that aims to protect the country's core interests.

B.   Implications for Current U.S. Security Commitments to Europe and NATO

The political agenda of the 2016 Trump campaign, as well as the first days of the administration, mirrored similar debates of the past. Thus, this section extracts certain themes of President Trump's foreign policy and considers whether those themes are a consistent with the history and practice of U.S. statecraft. The goal of this analysis is to assess the potential implications of its past foreign policy decisions on America's security commitments to Europe and NATO in the near term.

1.   Rhetoric of the 2016 Election Campaign and the New Trump Administration

In 2016, President Donald J. Trump entered the political stage as the Republican presidential candidate with a clear message. He wanted to develop a new foreign policy for the United States and repeatedly distinguished himself from the political establishment in Washington. Trump wanted "to shake the rust off America's foreign policy."[568] In his eyes, the post-Cold War policy was lacking a clear vision, caused

---

[568] Trump, "Trump on Foreign Policy."

constant policy disasters, and had major deficiencies such as overstretched resources, unfair burden sharing, unreliability of foreign policy, lack of seriousness, and lack of clear goals.[569]

Based on an interest-driven policy with mercantile, if not mercenary, overtones, Trump, as far as NATO is concerned, wanted to rebalance financial commitments among allies to the benefit of the United States and reform the alliance's outdated mission and structure to counter challenges such as migration and Islamic terrorism—if necessary with military force.[570] U.S. security and economic interests thereby dominate his thinking: "America First will be the major and overriding theme of my administration," he said.[571] Hence, the debate about the country's role in the concert of nations and the relationship to NATO, particularly burden sharing, were back on the table.

On February 23, 2017, chief White House strategist Steve Bannon said that the president "is 'maniacally focused' on fulfilling his campaign pledges."[572] Thus, Trump transferred his promises into policy and laid out his strategy in a joint address to Congress on February 28, 2017. Concerning foreign policy, the president emphasized America's readiness to lead and announced a significant increase in defense spending to provide the tools for preventing war but also the means for fighting and winning a conflict when it would be necessary to keep America safe.[573] Trump further asserted that "foreign policy calls for a direct, robust and meaningful engagement with the world. It is American leadership based on vital security interests that we share with our

---

[569] Trump, "Trump on Foreign Policy."

[570] Ibid.

[571] Ibid.

[572] See David Smith and Sabrina Siddiqui, "Steve Bannon: Trump Is 'Maniacally Focused' on Executing Promises," *Guardian*, February 23, 2017, https://www.theguardian.com/us-news/2017/feb/23/steve-bannon-cpac donald-trump-media-campaign-pledges.

[573] Donald J. Trump, "Remarks by President Trump in Joint Address to Congress," Office of the Press Secretary, White House, February 28, 2017, https://www.whitehouse.gov/the-press-office/2017/02/28/remarks-president-trump-joint-address-congress.

allies across the globe"; in this context, he promised to seek cooperation to extinguish Islamic terrorism "from our planet."[574]

Trump, however, is also willing to take unilateral action, if he deems it necessary. For instance, he ordered a cruise missile attack on a Syrian airfield on April 7, 2017, as a retaliation for a poison gas attack on civilians. The U.S. response was "just a small representation of our military's overall capability and a fraction of what this President will continue to build up the military to be throughout his administration," Trump's speaker Sean Spicer said.[575] On April 13, 2017, for the first time, the United States dropped the largest non-nuclear bomb in its arsenals, a GBU-43 weapon, on Taliban positions in Afghanistan.[576] Despite the questionable operational need for using such a large bomb, this attack sent a powerful signal to the world amid a worsening conflict with North Korea about its aggressive nuclear and missile programs. In short words, despite relentless criticism during the election campaign, Trump follows a clear interventionist policy in the use of military force and is willing to employ all necessary means when it contributes to U.S. interests.

Interestingly, neither Trump's inauguration address nor his first joint address to Congress included common values as a binding element of transatlantic partnership. The president strongly supports NATO, but the partners would need to fulfill their financial obligations; recent pressure had already shown first positive results—a comment that reveals his strategy toward NATO.[577] At the 2017 Munich Security Conference, Secretary of Defense James Norman Mattis clarified the U.S. position and stated that the United States would adhere to NATO since it is the best way to address security issues for the Western nations. Nevertheless, all those who benefit from the "best alliance in the

---

[574] Trump, "Remarks by President Trump in Joint Address to Congress."

[575] Sean Spicer, "Daily Press Briefing by Press Secretary Sean Spicer," Office of the Press Secretary, White House, April 10, 2017, https://www.whitehouse.gov/the-press-office/2017/04/10/daily-press-briefing-press-secretary-sean-spicer-35.

[576] Sean Spicer, "Daily Press Briefing by Press Secretary Sean Spicer," Office of the Press Secretary, White House, April 13, 2017, https://www.whitehouse.gov/the-press-office/2017/04/13/daily-press-briefing-press-secretary-spicer-37.

[577] Trump, "Remarks by President Trump in Joint Address to Congress."

world" should pay the necessary costs to defend freedom.[578] That is to say, the United States wants to strengthen its leadership role and more closely tie in NATO in the fight for U.S. security interests. Consequently, security guarantees for Europe might become a bargaining chip for pressing the allies to higher defense expenditures and widening NATO's portfolio.

Concerning the economy, Trump criticized excessive overseas spending and high debts instead of investing in U.S. infrastructure; thus, he expects a $1 trillion infrastructure program, financed through public and private money, to revitalize the economy and diminish unemployment.[579] Furthermore, the president promised to lower taxes for the middle class and industry and to fight against unfair taxation of U.S. goods. No one should any longer take advantage of U.S. companies and workers: "buy American, hire American," he said.[580] Trump also envisaged reducing the enormous balance of trade deficit, which reached almost $800 billion in 2016, and he called for bipartisanship in solving the pressing economic challenges to "restart the engine of the American economy."[581] In Trump's perception, the country is in an economic crisis, which requires extreme measures to revitalize the domestic market. In short, the president's vision of the U.S. economy is one of mercantilism, protectionism, and "America First." Trade partners should pay tribute to the United States and de-emphasize their own economic interests for the sake of a favorable balance of payments relationship.

2. Continuities and Discontinuities

As the analysis of the case studies showed, domestic policy—to a high degree—determines U.S. foreign policy. President Trump has made the

---

[578] James Norman Mattis, "Remarks by Secretary Mattis at the Munich Security Conference in Munich, Germany," U.S. Department of Defense, February 17, 2017, https://www.defense.gov/News/Speeches/Speech View/Article/1087838/remarks-by-secretary-mattis-at-the-munich-security-conference-in-munich-germany.

[579] Trump, "Remarks by President Trump in Joint Address to Congress."

[580] Ibid.

[581] Ibid.

revitalization of the U.S. economy his main concern and proposed a huge investment program to modernize infrastructure and reduce unemployment. The specter of economic decline has repeatedly appeared in U.S. history. In the 20th century, the United States confronted two world wars, the Great Depression in the 1930s, demobilization after the Second World War, and numerous regional wars such as in Korea and Vietnam. Compared to the severe economic and societal problems of the past, though, Trump's presidency starts from a quite comfortable situation.

To be sure, America faces serious problems such as the huge balance of payments deficit and the debts issue. However, Trump is not planning to solve the debt crisis by reductions in defense spending because just recently he promised significant increases of the military budget. Nor did the president officially announce a reduction in the balance-of-payments issue by pressing the Europeans to reimburse U.S. defense efforts as was the case in the 1960s and 1970s.

Such a strategy, however, might become part of his policy toward NATO. For instance, in a Tweet following the visit of German Chancellor Angela Merkel on March 17, 2017, Trump claimed that "Germany owes vast sums of money to NATO & the United States must be paid more for the powerful, and very expensive, defense it provides to Germany!"[582] The presentation of such a bill would almost exactly mirror U.S. pressure on NATO during the Johnson and Nixon administrations. At that time, Germany solved the problem with its checkbook. But, are the Europeans willing to pay today?

In the Mansfield era, the Senate called for U.S. troop reductions in Europe and fair burden sharing, and demanded to spend the savings on domestic issues (i.e., social programs) or at least ease the costs of the Vietnam War. Increased European defense spending was a way to reduce the U.S. share of the (relatively predictable) costs of European defense against the Warsaw Pact. Trump, however, has not announced such plans yet. So, why then should NATO spend more on defense?

---

[582] Quoted in Amanda Erikson, "No, Germany Doesn't Owe America 'Vast Sums' of Money for NATO," *Washington Post*, March 18, 2017, https://www.washingtonpost.com/news/worldviews/wp/2017/03/18/no-germany-doesnt-owe-america-vast-sums-of-money-for-nato/?utm_term=.5e8de72f4992.

One should remember Kissinger's 1973 to-the-point statement that European interests are regional whereas U.S. interests are global. Trump shares the Farewell Address' suspicion about other nations' influence on the "establishment" in Washington and claims to be willing to avoid foreign manipulation.[583] Ironically, Trump's plans to change NATO's operational focus to a worldwide war on Islamic terrorism could actually increase the demand for a European Farewell Address, since the NATO allies now risk being pressed into U.S. conflicts—even though these conflicts might be outside of Europe's regional focus and the national interests of the European partners. As a result, it is understandable that Europe may not necessarily cheer about Trump's policy.

Trump follows the general opinion of the U.S. public. During the election campaign, Trump's rhetoric included some uncertainness about his position toward NATO, and arguments for retrenchment became strong. Upon taking office, the president emphasized his strong support for the alliance. Concerns that the United States might adopt a neutrality policy turned out to be unfounded. Although in the past public support for an active foreign policy could not be taken for granted (i.e., prior to the Second World War, until Pearl Harbor, 1941), today an overwhelming majority supports an active U.S. foreign policy. For instance, recent polls revealed that 95 percent of the U.S. public supports an active role in world affairs, of which 13 percent say that the United States should be the single world leader.[584] Nine out of ten Americans think that the United States should remain a member of NATO.[585] A large majority, however, also expresses reservations about America's dominant role and thinks that the United States is doing more than its fair share.[586] Trump's policy follows these public trends. Thus, America accepts its self-imposed leadership role but lays stronger emphasis on national interests and making good deals.

---

[583] Donald J. Trump, "The Inaugural Address," Office of the Press Secretary, White House, January 20, 2017, https://www.whitehouse.gov/inaugural-address.

[584] See Steven Kull, "Americans on the U.S. Role in the World: A Study of U.S. Public Attitudes," University of Maryland, January 2017, 3, http://www.public-consultation.org/wp-content/uploads/2017/01/PPC_Role_in_World_Report.pdf.

[585] Kull, "Americans on the U.S. Role in the World," 5.

[586] Ibid., 4.

Concerning the economy, Trump secures his sphere of interest. The plans to revitalize the U.S. economy are based on a mercantile "America first" strategy as it existed in the 1930s, when the United States protected its markets with high tariffs and taxes, or in the early 1970s, when tariffs were expected to compensate the balance of payments deficit. Washington's Farewell Address advocates free trade "neither seeking nor granting exclusive favors or preferences [and] consulting the natural course of things."[587] Historically, U.S. economic expansionism was in many cases best supported by a policy of extensive investments in foreign markets (i.e., Dawes and Young Plan, Truman Doctrine, Marshall Plan). Free trade and the freedom of the seas even played a huge role at the dawn of both world wars. Hence, one might raise some doubts about a new economic protectionism in a globalized world economy.

3. Final Remarks

This volume sought to investigate the roots of isolationist and internationalist sentiments, which were only poorly reflected in public debate during the 2016 presidential election campaign. Much of the rhetoric ramified into elements of isolationist traditions. By contrast, domestic and partisan politics dominated the debates, and criticism of foreign politics was just a tool to sharpen the candidate's profile as a man of action. Since Trump has committed to stick to his campaign promises, it is likely that the president envisages a much more realist policy focusing on economy and security and searching for short-term deals instead of long-term gains, especially on economic issues.

The pendulum of foreign policy, however, will not swing to the extreme of isolationism and disentanglement from European affairs as seen in the 1920s and 1930s. Trump's current interest in NATO primarily limits itself to the question of fair burden sharing. The test for the U.S. support of the alliance will be the willingness of the European allies to join Trump's plans for a global war on Islamic terrorism. To reach this goal and impose his will on NATO, Trump will not shy away from using the threat of retrenchment from U.S. security commitments

---

[587] Washington, "Farewell Address."

to Europe. Thus, European NATO allies should prepare themselves for strong rhetoric and attacks in the future.

Trump's presidency is yet too new to render a verdict on whether it will constitute a major shift in the U.S. internationalist policy pursued since the Second World War. I assume the answer is "No," but an *ex-post* analysis will show the impact of his new mercantilist approach. Nevertheless, the dispute about a forward, engaged policy versus a more neutral, inward directed one will outlast Trump's presidency and remain a part of U.S. political debates.

APPENDIX

The U.S. geographic location in the western hemisphere and its position in the international community, for a long time, determined the conduct of U.S. foreign policy. Doris A. Graber explains that U.S. foreign policy since the early 19th century followed three mandates: first, deter European nations from intervening on the American continent; second, reject any pressure on the U.S. government from the outside; third, establish a moral component in foreign policy as a psychological tool against undesirable international conduct.[588] The United States usually saw foreign involvement as an undesired option; thus, any decision to intervene was always controversial.[589]

This approach to foreign policy was challenged by the two world wars and the emergence of the Cold War, but much of this old thinking is still present. This appendix depicts some key expressions of isolationism and anti-isolationism in U.S. foreign policy—Washington's Farewell Address, the Monroe Doctrine, and Kennan's Containment policy.

A.   Washington's Farewell Address

With the Farewell Address in 1796, retiring U.S. President George Washington set foreign policy principles to preserve the nation's freedom of action. At the end of the 18th century, the United States confronted European *realpolitik* of fragile alliances and the French Revolutionary Wars (1792–1803). Historian Felix Gilbert explains that, when in 1793 Britain, Holland, and Spain joined the war of the German Powers against France, the French wanted the Unites States to join on their side because of the 1778 Franco-American alliance.[590] Because British and Spanish colonies surrounded the country on the American continent and the British were able to blockade trade lines, a conflict with

---

[588] Doris A. Graber, "Intervention and Nonintervention," in *Encyclopedia of American Foreign Affairs*, 2nd ed., ed. Alexander DeConde, Richard Dean Burns, and Frederik Logevall (New York: Scribner, 2002), 315.

[589] Ibid., 334.

[590] Felix Gilbert, *To the Farewell Address: Ideas of Early American Foreign Policy* (Princeton, NJ: Princeton University Press, 1961), 116–17.

the Europeans could easily affect U.S. economic interests, which encouraged President Washington to answer with a proclamation of neutrality as the only way to preserve freedom of action.[591] In his 1796 Farewell Address, Washington announced, "Our country, under all the circumstances of the case, had a right to take ... a neutral position. Having taken it, I determined, as far as should depend upon me, to maintain it, with moderation, perseverance, and firmness."[592] Herring concludes that the Farewell Address shows U.S. fears of getting involved in European intrigues and thus became the first comprehensive statement to guide the nation's foreign policy in its formative years.[593]

Washington also warned that alliances might draw the country into wars without justification and without any benefit beyond simply defending the partner; hence, America should "steer clear of permanent alliances," which were only acceptable under "extraordinary emergencies."[594] Furthermore, the president explained that "Europe has a set of primary interests which to us have none. ... It must be unwise in us to implicate ourselves by artificial ties in the ordinary vicissitudes of her politics."[595] Washington portrays those who further others' interests as the "tools and dupes" of foreign nations, usurping the applause and confidence of the American people though surrendering American interests, while the "real patriots who may resist the intrigues ... become suspected and odious."[596]

Herring summarizes that U.S. exceptionalist principles and a favorable geography caused a strong belief that the country could best achieve success when it insisted on its freedom of action.[597] Thus, for the young nation, any entanglements, especially in European affairs, were not in its interest, and Americans had to avoid any binding political commitments, not wage war, and remain neutral.

---

[591] Gilbert, *To the Farewell Address*, 116–17.
[592] Washington, "Farewell Address."
[593] Herring, *From Colony to Superpower*, 83.
[594] Washington, "Farewell Address."
[595] Ibid.
[596] Ibid.
[597] Herring, *From Colony to Superpower*, 83.

B. The Monroe Doctrine

By the early 1820s, Spanish and Portuguese colonies in Latin America had achieved or were close to achieving independence. According to Herring, at the Congress of Verona in 1822 the alliance of the monarchies of Austria, Prussia, and Russia—who had previously formed the Holy Alliance at the Congress of Vienna in 1815—and France decided to restore Spanish monarchy and its Latin American colonies or establish independent puppet monarchies.[598] The United States had taken a neutral position toward the Latin American revolutions and hoped for trade advantages from emerging Latin America.[599] Alarmed by the possibility of European intervention, President James Monroe needed to take action.

The later so-called Monroe Doctrine was part of the president's 1823 annual message to Congress. It secured spheres of influence, warned European powers not to conduct further colonization in the western hemisphere, and stated U.S. disinterest in European affairs. Monroe urged that "we should consider any attempt on their part to extend their system to any portion of this hemisphere as dangerous to our peace and safety."[600] Monroe's basic intent was to meet major concerns about the country's Latin American backyard, but he further declared, "Our policy in regard to Europe … is not to interfere in the internal concerns of any of its powers."[601] Monroe asserted the two separate spheres of influence of the Old and the New World and a non-colonization and a non-intervention policy. This course was the core principle for U.S. foreign policy until 1917.

C. George F. Kennan's Containment Policy

Following the Second World War, America saw a major shift in the conduct of foreign policy. In the light of the incipient Cold War, Kennan, with his famous 1947 "Mr. X" article, "The Sources of Soviet

---

[598] Herring, *From Colony to Superpower*, 153.

[599] Ibid., 154.

[600] Monroe, "Annual Message to Congress."

[601] Ibid.

Conduct," searched for a path between peace and war, avoiding potentially deathly outcomes. Kennan's perception of the Soviet Union expressed deep mistrust, and he warned that the conflict between the blocs was foremost a clash of mutually exclusive ideologies.[602] He stated, "The United States need only measure up to its own best traditions and prove itself worthy of preservation as a great nation," and the challenge to the American people would be to pull "themselves together and ... [accept] the responsibilities of moral and political leadership that history plainly intended them to bear."[603] Hence, Kennan assumed that humility in foreign policy would have much greater effects on the outcome of the Cold War than a shortsighted preoccupation with military solutions. He repeated this view during the Korean War with his 1951 article "America and the Russian Future," explaining that "the most important influence that the United States can bring ... will continue to be influence of example."[604] America should accept its imposed leadership role. Kennan's policy of leadership through example and the skepticism about military means alone in U.S. diplomacy constituted a school of thought and practice in statecraft for decades.

---

[602] Kennan, *American Diplomacy*, 95.

[603] Ibid., 106.

[604] Ibid., 126–27.

LIST OF REFERENCES

Acheson, Dean. *Present at the Creation: My Years in the State Department.* New York: Norton, 1969.

Ambrosius, Lloyd E. *Woodrow Wilson and the American Diplomatic Tradition: The Treaty Fight in Perspective.* New York: Cambridge University Press, 1987.

Bailey, Thomas A. *Woodrow Wilson & The Great Betrayal.* New York: Quadrangle, 1945.

———. *Woodrow Wilson & The Lost Peace.* Chicago: Quadrangle, 1944.

Baylis, John. *The Diplomacy of Pragmatism.* Basingstoke, UK: Palgrave Macmillan, 1993.

Beard, Charles Austin. *American Foreign Policy in the Making, 1932–1940: A Study in Responsibilities.* New Haven: Yale University Press, 1946.

Bevin, Ernest. "Address Given to the House of Commons." University of Luxembourg. January 22, 1948. http://www.cvce.eu/content/publication/2002/9/9/7bc0ecbd-c50e-4035-8e36-ed70bfbd204c/publishable_en.pdf.

Binder, L. James. *Lemnitzer: A Soldier for His Time.* Washington, DC: Brassey's, 1997.

Bullock, Alan. *Ernest Bevin: Foreign Secretary 1945–1951.* New York: W.W. Norton, 1983.

Churchill, Winston. "The Sinews of Peace." The International Churchill Society. March 5, 1946. http://www.winstonchurchill.org/resources/speeches/1946-1963-elder-statesman/120-the-sinews-of-peace.

Cohen, Warren I. *The Cambridge History of American Foreign Relations: America in the Age of Soviet Power, 1945–1991.* New York: Cambridge University Press, 1993.

Cole, Wayne S. *America First: The Battle against Intervention, 1940–1941.* New York: Octagon Books, 1971.

Columbia Law Review. "The Johnson Act: Extension of Credit to a Government in Default," 35, no. 1 (1935): 102–4. doi:10.2307/1116369.

Conn, Stetson, Byron Fairchild, and Center of Military History. *The Framework of Hemisphere Defense*. Washington, DC: U.S. Army Center of Military History, 1989.

Craig, Gordon A., and Alexander L. George. *Force and Statecraft: Diplomatic Problems of Our Time*. 3rd ed. New York: Oxford University Press, 1995.

Dallek, Robert. *Franklin D. Roosevelt and American Foreign Policy, 1932–1945*. New York: Oxford University Press, 1979.

Doenecke, Justus D. *Storm on the Horizon: The Challenge to American Intervention, 1939–1941*. New York: Rowman & Littlefield, 2003.

Dumbrell, John. "American Isolationism: A Response to David Hastings Dunn." *Review of International Studies*, 31, no. 4 (2005): 699–700. doi:10.1017/S0260210505006704.

———. "Varieties of Post-Cold War American Isolationism." *Government and Opposition* 34 (1999): 24-43. doi:10.1111/j.1477-7053.1999.tb00469.x.

Dunn, David Hastings. "Isolationism Revisited: Seven Persistent Myths in the Contemporary American Foreign Policy Debate." *Review of International Studies* 31, no. 2 (2005): 237–61. doi:10.10171S0260210505006431.

Duroselle, Jean-Baptiste. *From Wilson to Roosevelt: Foreign Policy of the United States 1913-1945*. Cambridge: Harvard University Press, 1963.

Erikson, Amanda. "No, Germany Doesn't Owe America 'Vast Sums' of Money for NATO." *Washington Post*, March 18, 2017. https://www.washingtonpost.com/news/worldviews/wp/2017/03/18/no-germany-doesnt-owe-america-vast-sums-of-money-for-nato/?utm_term=.5e8de72f4992.

Ferrell, Robert Hugh. *Peace in Their Time: The Origins of the Kellogg-Briand Pact*. New Haven: Yale University Press, 1952.

Fisher, Max, and Amanda Taub. "How Donald Trump Hacked the Politics of Foreign Policy." *New York Times*, October 19, 2016. http://www.nytimes.com/2016/10/20/world/americas/donald-trump-foreign-policy.html?ref=world&_r=0.

Flores, Reena. "Newt Gingrich: NATO Countries 'Ought to Worry' about U.S. Commitment," *CBS News*, July 21, 2016. http://www.cbsnews.com/news/newt-gingrich-trump-would-reconsider-his-obligation-to-nato/.

Frieden, Jeffry A. *Global Capitalism: Its Fall and Rise in the Twentieth Century*. New York: Norton, 2006.

Gaddis, John Lewis. *Strategies of Containment: A Critical Appraisal of Postwar American Security Policy*. New York: Oxford University Press, 1982.

Gearan, Anne. "Clinton Slams Trump as a Dangerous Isolationist in American Legion Speech." *Washington Post*, August 31, 2016. https://www.washingtonpost.com/news/post-politics/wp/2016/08/31/clinton-plans-to-slam-trump-as-a-dangerous-isolationist-in-american-legion-speech/.

Gilbert, Felix. *To the Farewell Address: Ideas of Early American Foreign Policy*. Princeton, NJ: Princeton University Press, 1961.

Golden, James R. *NATO Burden-sharing: Risks and Opportunities*. New York: Praeger, 1982.

Graber, Doris A. "Intervention and Nonintervention." In *Encyclopedia of American Foreign Affairs*, 2nd ed., edited by Alexander DeConde, Richard Dean Burns, and Frederik Logevall, 315-35, New York: Scribner, 2002.

Hanhimäki, Jussi M. "Global Visions and Parochial Politics: The Persistent Dilemma of the 'American Century.'" *Diplomatic History* 27, no. 4 (2003): 423–47. ProQuest (60671679).

Harper, John Lamberton. *American Visions of Europe*. New York: Cambridge University Press, 1996.

Herring, George C. *From Colony to Superpower: U.S. Foreign Relations Since 1776*. New York: Oxford University Press, 2008.

Hoover, Herbert. "Special Message to the Congress on Intergovernmental Debts and International Economic Conditions." American Presidency Project. University of California. December 19, 1932. http://www.presidency.ucsb.edu/ws/index.php?pid=23390&st=debts&st1=.

Hoover, Herbert. "Statement on Signing the Foreign Debt Moratorium Resolution." American Presidency Project. University of California. December 23, 1931. http://www.presidency.ucsb.edu/ws/?pid=22955.

Ireland, Timothy P. *Creating the Entangling Alliance: The Origins of the North Atlantic Treaty Organization.* Westport: Greenwood, 1981.

Johnson, Arthur Menzies. *The American Economy: An Historical Introduction to the Problems of the 1970's.* New York: Free Press, 1974.

Johnson, Lyndon Baines. *The Vantage Point: Perspectives of the Presidency 1963-1969.* New York: Holt, Rinehart and Winston, 1971.

Jonas, Manfred. "Isolationism." In *Encyclopedia of American Foreign Affairs*, 2nd ed., edited by Alexander DeConde, Richard Dean Burns, and Frederik Logevall, 337–51. New York: Scribner, 2002.

———. *Isolationism in America, 1935-1941.* New York: Cornell University Press, 1966.

Kaplan, Lawrence S. *Recent American Foreign Policy: Conflicting Interpretations.* Homewood, IL: Dorsey, 1968.

———. *The United States and NATO: The Formative Years.* Lexington: University Press of Kentucky, 1984.

Kay, Sean. *NATO and the Future of European Security.* Lanham, MD: Rowman & Littlefield, 1998.

Kennan, George F. "Long Telegram." The National Security Archive. George Washington University. February 22, 1946. http://nsarchive.gwu.edu/coldwar/documents/episode-1/kennan.htm.

———. *American Diplomacy 1900-1950.* Chicago: University of Chicago Press, 1951.

Kissinger, Henry "8. Address by the President's Assistant for National Security Affairs." Office of the Historian. Bureau of Public Affairs. United States Department of State. April 23, 1973. https://history.state.gov/historicaldocuments/frus1969-76v38p1/d8.

———. *White House Years.* Boston: Little, Brown and Co., 1979.

Knock, Thomas J. *To End All Wars: Woodrow Wilson and the Quest for a New World Order.* New York: Oxford University Press, 1992.

Kull, Steven. "Americans on the U.S. Role in the World: A Study of U.S. Public Attitudes." University of Maryland. January 2017, 3. http://www.publicconsultation.org/wp-content/uploads/2017/01/PPC_Role_in_World_Report.pdf.

Langer, William Leonard, and Sarell Everett Gleason. *The Challenge to Isolation, 1937-1940.* New York: Harper, 1952.

Link, Arthur Stanley. *Wilson: Campaigns for Progressivism and Peace 1916-17.* Princeton, NJ: Princeton University Press, 1965.

———. *Wilson: The Struggle for Neutrality 1914-15.* Princeton, NJ: Princeton University Press, 1960.

———. *Woodrow Wilson and the Progressive Era 1910-1917.* New York: Harper & Brothers, 1954.

Mansfield, Michael J. "Central Concerns of American Foreign Policy." Montana Memory Project. Montana State Library. March 13, 1967. http://mtmemory.org/cdm/singleitem/collection/p16013coll41/id/1391/rec/726.

Marshall, George C. "The 'Marshall Plan' Speech." Organization for Economic Cooperation and Development. June 5, 1947. http://www.oecd.org/general/themarshallplanspeechatharvarduniversity5june1947.htm.

Mattis, James Norman. "Remarks by Secretary Mattis at the Munich Security Conference in Munich, Germany." U.S. Department of Defense. February 17, 2017. https://www.defense.gov/News/Speeches/Speech-View/Article/1087838/remarks-by-secretary-mattis-at-the-munich-security-conference-in-munich-germany.

McCullough, David. *Truman.* New York: Simon & Schuster, 1992.

McNamara, Robert S. *In Retrospect: The Tragedy and Lessons of Vietnam.* New York: Times Books, 1995.

Monroe, James. "Annual Message to Congress." 100 Milestone Documents. U.S. National Archives and Records Administration. December 2, 1823. https://www.ourdocuments.gov/doc.php?flash=true&doc=23&page=transcript.

Nelson, C. Richard. *The Life and Work of General Andrew J. Goodpaster: Best Practices in National Security Affairs*. Lanham, MD: Rowman & Littlefield, 2016.

Nitze, Paul H. S., Nelson Drew, and National Defense University. *NSC-68: Forging the Strategy of Containment*. Washington: National Defense University, 1994.

Nixon, Richard. "U.S. Foreign Policy for the 1970s: A New Strategy for Peace." Office of the Historian. Bureau of Public Affairs. United States Department of State. February 18, 1970. https://history.state.gov/historicaldocuments/frus1969-76v01/d60.

North Atlantic Treaty Organization. "Final Communiqué." e-Library. May, 28, 1969. http://www.nato.int/cps/en/natohq/official_texts_26765.htm?selectedLocale=en.

———. *NATO Basic Documents*. Brussels: NATO Information Service, 1976.

Office of the Historian. "The Dawes Plan, the Young Plan, German Reparations, and Inter-allied War Debts." United States Department of State. Accessed March 8, 2017. https://history.state.gov/milestones/1921-1936/dawes.

Pedlow, Gregory W. "NATO Strategy Documents 1949-1969." Historical Office. Supreme Headquarters Allied Powers Europe. 1999. http://www.nato.int/docu/stratdoc/eng/intro.pdf.

Pois, Anne Marie. "The U.S. Women's International League for Peace and Freedom and American Neutrality, 1935–1939." *Peace & Change* 14, no. 3 (1989): 263–84.

Ravenhill, John. *Global Political Economy*. 4th ed. Oxford, UK: Oxford University Press, 2014.

Reynolds, David. *From Munich to Pearl Harbor: Roosevelt's America and the Origins of the Second World War*. Chicago: Ivan R. Dee, 2001.

Roosevelt, Franklin Delano. "Fireside Chat." American Presidency Project. University of California. December 29, 1940. http://www.presidency.ucsb.edu/ws/?pid=15917.

Roosevelt, Franklin Delano. "Fireside Chat." American Presidency Project. University of California. September 11, 1941. http://www.presidency.ucsb.edu/ws/?pid=16012.

———. "Inaugural Address." American Presidency Project. University of California. March 4, 1933. http://www.presidency.ucsb.edu/ws/?pid=14473.

———. "Press Conference." American Presidency Project. University of California. December 17, 1940. http://www.presidency.ucsb.edu/ws/?pid=15913.

———. "Radio Address Announcing an Unlimited National Emergency." American Presidency Project. University of California. May 27, 1941. http://www.presidency.ucsb.edu/ws/?pid=16120.

———. "Appeal for World Peace by Disarmament and for Relief from Economic Chaos." American Presidency Project. University of California. May 16, 1933. http://www.presidency.ucsb.edu/ws/index.php?pid=14643.

———. "Campaign Address at Boston." American Presidency Project. University of California. October 30, 1940, http://www.presidency.ucsb.edu/ws/?pid=15887.

———. "Fireside Chat." American Presidency Project. University of California. September 3, 1939. http://www.presidency.ucsb.edu/ws/?pid=15801.

———. "Message to the Senate in re World Court." FDR Library's Digital Collections. University of Illinois. January 16, 1935. http://www.fdrlibrary.marist.edu/_resources/images/msf/msf00781.

———. "President Franklin Roosevelt's Annual Message to Congress." 100 Milestone Documents. U.S. National Archives and Records Administration. January 9, 1941. https://www.ourdocuments.gov/doc.php?doc=70&page=transcript.

———. "Quarantine Speech." Miller Center. University of Virginia. October 5, 1937, http://millercenter.org/president/speeches/speech-3310.

Roosevelt, Franklin Delano. "Speech to New York State Grange." FDR Library's Digital Collections. University of Illinois. February 2, 1932. http://www.fdrlibrary.marist.edu/_resources/images/msf/msf00470.

———. "Statement on Neutrality Legislation." American Presidency Project. University of California. August 31, 1935. http://www.presidency.ucsb.edu/ws/index.php?pid=14927.

———. "Wireless to the London Conference." American Presidency Project. University of California. July 3, 1933. http://www.presidency.ucsb.edu/ws/?pid=14679.

Rosenberg, Samuel. *American Economic Development since 1945*. Gordonsville, VA: Palgrave Macmillan, 2003.

S. Kaplan, Lawrence. *Recent American Foreign Policy: Conflicting Interpretations*. Homewood, IL: Dorsey, 1968.

Schwartz, James Edmond. "Senator Michael J. Mansfield and United States Military Disengagement from Europe: A Case Study in American Foreign Policy: The Majority Leader, His Amendment, and His Influence upon the Senate." PhD diss., University of North Carolina, 1977.

Sestanovich, Stephen. "Are U.S. Voters Becoming Isolationist–or Just More Partisan?" *Wall Street Journal* (blog). October 11, 2016. http://blogs.wsj.com/washwire/2016/10/11/are-u-s-voters-becoming-isolationist-or-just-more-partisan/.

Small, Melvin. *Democracy & Diplomacy: The Impact of Domestic Politics on U.S. Foreign Policy 1789-1994*. Baltimore: John Hopkins University Press, 1996.

Smith, David, and Sabrina Siddiqui. "Steve Bannon: Trump is 'Maniacally Focused' on Executing Promises." *Guardian*, February 23, 2017. https://www.theguardian.com/us-news/2017/feb/23/steve-bannon-cpac-donald-trump-media-campaign-pledges.

Spicer, Sean. "Daily Press Briefing by Press Secretary Sean Spicer." Office of the Press Secretary. White House. April 10, 2017. https://www.whitehouse.gov/the-press-office/2017/04/10/daily-press-briefing-press-secretary-sean-spicer-35.

Spicer, Sean. "Daily Press Briefing by Press Secretary Sean Spicer." Office of the Press Secretary. White House. April 13, 2017, https://www.whitehouse.gov/the-press-office/2017/04/13/daily-press-briefing-press-secretary-spicer-37.

Stalin, Joseph. "Stalin Election Speech." Seventeen Moments in Soviet History. Michigan State University. February 9, 1946. http://soviethistory.msu.edu/1947-2/cold-war/cold-war-texts/stalin-election-speech/.

Stewart, Richard W. *The Korean War: The Chinese Intervention.* Washington, DC: U.S. Army Center of Military History, 2000.

Thies, Wallace J. *Why NATO Endures.* New York: Cambridge University Press, 2009.

Thomas, Ian Q. R. *The Promise of Alliance: NATO and the Political Imagination.* Lanham, MD: Rowman & Littlefield, 1997.

Tierney, Dominic. *FDR and the Spanish Civil War: Neutrality and Commitment in the Struggle that Divided America.* London: Duke, 2007.

Trachtenberg, Marc. *A Constructed Peace: The Making of the European Settlement 1945-1963.* Princeton, NJ: Princeton University Press, 1999.

———. *The Craft of International History: A Guide to Method.* Princeton, NJ: Princeton University Press, 2006.

Truman, Harry S. "Special Message to the Congress Presenting a 21-Point Program for the Reconversion Period." American Presidency Project. University of California. September 6, 1945. http://www.presidency.ucsb.edu/ws/?pid=12359.

———. "Address Before a Joint Session of Congress." Avalon Project. Yale Law School. March 12, 1947. http://avalon.law.yale.edu/20th_century/trudoc.asp.

———. "Special Message to the Congress on the Threat to the Freedom of Europe." American Presidency Project. University of California. March 17, 1948. http://www.presidency.ucsb.edu/ws/?pid=13130.

Truman, Harry S. "The President's News Conference." American Presidency Project. University of California. January 11, 1951. http://www.presidency.ucsb.edu/ws/index.php?pid=14050.

———. "The President's News Conference." American Presidency Project. University of California. January 18, 1951. http://www.presidency.ucsb.edu/ws/index.php?pid=13843.

Trump, Donald J. "Remarks by President Trump in Joint Address to Congress." Office of the Press Secretary. White House. February 28, 2017. https://www.whitehouse.gov/the-press-office/2017/02/28/remarks-president-trump-joint-address-congress.

———. "The Inaugural Address." Office of the Press Secretary. White House. January 20, 2017. https://www.whitehouse.gov/inaugural-address.

———. "Trump on Foreign Policy." *National Interest.* April 27, 2016. http://nationalinterest.org/feature/trump-foreign-policy-15960.

United States Department of State. *Peace and War: United States Foreign Policy, 1931-1941.* Washington, DC: GPO, 1943.

United States Senate. Committee on Foreign Relations and Committee on Armed Services. *Assignment of Ground Forces of the United States to Duty in the European Area on S. Res. 8*, United States Senate, 82nd Cong., 1st sess. Washington, DC: GPO, 1951.

———. Committee on Foreign Relations. *First Session on Executive L, the North Atlantic Treaty. Part I: Administration Witnesses*, United States Senate, 81st Cong., 1st sess. Washington, DC: GPO, 1949.

U.S. National Archives and Records Administration. "Land Lease Bill." 100 Milestone Documents. March 11, 1941. https://www.ourdocuments.gov/doc.php?doc=71&page=transcript.

———. "Tonkin Gulf Resolution." 100 Milestone Documents. January 7, 1964. https://ourdocuments.gov/doc.php?doc=98&page=transcript.

Walker, Douglas Earl. "The Phoenix of Foreign Policy: Isolationism's Influence on U.S. Foreign Policy during the Twentieth Century." Master's thesis, Naval Postgraduate School, 1992.

Washington, George. "Farewell Address." 100 Milestone Documents. U.S. National Archives and Records Administration. September 19, 1796. https://www.ourdocuments.gov/doc.php?doc=15&page=transcript.

Wiebes, Cees, and Bert Zeeman. "The Pentagon Negotiations March 1948: The Launching of the North Atlantic Treaty." *International Affairs* 59, no. 3 (1983): 351–63.

Williams, Phil. *The Senate and U.S. Troops in Europe*. New York: St. Martin's, 1985.

———. "What Happened to the Mansfield Amendment?" *Survival* 18, no. 4 (1976): 146–53. doi:10.1080/00396337608441623.

Wilson, Woodrow. "Statement Appealing to the Nation for Support in the 1918 Congressional Election." American Presidency Project. October 25, 1918. http://www.presidency.ucsb.edu/ws/?pid=110491.

———. "President Wilson's Declaration of War Message to Congress." 100 Milestone Documents. U.S. National Archives and Records Administration. April 2, 1917. https://www.ourdocuments.gov/doc.php?doc=62&page=transcript.

———. "President Woodrow Wilson's 14 Points." 100 Milestone Documents. U.S. National Archives and Records Administration. January 8, 1918. https://www.ourdocuments.gov/doc.php?doc=62&page=transcript.

Yale Law School. "The Covenant of the League of Nations." Avalon Project. December 1924. http://avalon.law.yale.edu/20th_century/leagcov.asp#art1.

Yost, David S. *NATO's Balancing Act*. Washington, DC: United States Institute of Peace, 2014.

Young, John W. *Britain, France, and the Unity of Europe, 1945–1951*. Leicester, UK: Leicester University Press, 1984.

Carola Hartmann Miles-Verlag

Politik, Gesellschaft, Militär

Uwe Hartmann, *Innere Führung. Erfolge und Defizite der Führungsphilosophie für die Bundeswehr,* Berlin 2007.

Reiner Pommerin (ed.), *Clausewitz goes global. Carl von Clausewitz in the 21st Century,* Berlin 2011.

Eberhard Birk, Winfried Heinemann, Sven Lange (Hrsg.), *Tradition für die Bundeswehr. Neue Aspekte einer alten Debatte,* Berlin 2012.

Angelika Dörfler-Dierken, *Führung in der Bundeswehr,* Berlin 2013.

Cornelia Fedtke, Kai-Uwe Hellmann, Jan Hörmann, *Migration und Militär. Zur Integration deutscher Soldaten mit Migrationshintergrund in der Bundeswehr,* Berlin 2013.

Wolf Graf von Baudissin, *Grundwert Frieden in Politik – Strategie – Führung von Streitkräften,* hrsg. von Claus von Rosen, Berlin 2014.

Wolf Graf von Baudissin, *Der Widerstand. „… um nie wieder in die ausweglose Lage zu geraten…",* hrsg. von Claus von Rosen, Berlin 2014.

Marcel Bohnert, Lukas J. Reitstetter (Hrsg.), *Armee im Aufbruch. Zur Gedankenwelt junger Offiziere in den Kampftruppen der Bundeswehr,* Berlin 2014.

Arjan Kozica, Kai Prüter, Hannes Wendroth (Hrsg.), *Unternehmen Bundeswehr? Theorie und Praxis (militärischer) Führung,* Berlin 2014.

Angelika Dörfler-Dierken, Robert Kramer, *Innere Führung in Zahlen. Streitkräftebefragung 2013,* Berlin 2014.

Phil C. Langer, Gerhard Kümmel (Hrsg.), *„Wir sind Bundeswehr." Wie viel Vielfalt benötigen/vertragen die Streitkräfte?,* Berlin 2015.

Dirk Freudenberg, *Counterinsurgency. Aufstandsbekämpfung als Phase zur Überwindung schwacher Staatlichkeit und zur Etablierung des Aufbaus einer stabilen Nachkriegsordnung?,* Berlin 2016.

Alois Bach, Walter Sauer (Hrsg.), *Schützen.Retten.Kämpfen. Dienen für Deutschland,* Berlin 2016.

Dirk Freudenberg, Stephan Maninger, *Neue Kriege. Sicherheitspolitische Rahmenbedingungen, Mentalitäten, Strategien, Methoden und Instrumente,* Berlin 2016.

Einsatzerfahrungen

Kay Kuhlen, *Um des lieben Friedens willen. Als Peacekeeper im Kosovo,* Eschede 2009.

Sascha Brinkmann, Joachim Hoppe (Hrsg.), *Generation Einsatz, Fallschirmjäger berichten ihre Erfahrungen aus Afghanistan,* Berlin 2010.

Artur Schwitalla, *Afghanistan, jetzt weiß ich erst… Gedanken aus meiner Zeit als Kommandeur des Provincial Reconstruction Team FEYZABAD,* Berlin 2010.

Uwe Hartmann, *War without Fighting? The Reintegration of Former Combatants in Afghanistan seen through the Lens of Strategic Thought,* Berlin 2014.

Rainer Buske, *KUNDUZ. Ein Erlebnisbericht über einen militärischen Einsatz der Bundeswehr in AFGHANISTAN im Jahre 2008,* Berlin ²2016.

Standpunkte und Orientierungen

Daniel Giese, *Militärische Führung im Internetzeitalter – Die Bedeutung von Strategischer Kommunikation und Social Media für Entscheidungsprozesse, Organisationsstrukturen und Führerausbildung in der Bundeswehr,* Berlin 2014.

Dirk Freudenberg, *Auftragstaktik und Innere Führung. Feststellungen und Anmerkungen zur Frage nach Bedeutung und Verhältnis des inneren Gefüges und der Auftragstaktik unter den Bedingungen des Einsatzes der Deutschen Bundeswehr,* Berlin 2014.

Uwe Hartmann (Hrsg.), *Lernen von Afghanistan. Innovative Mittel und Wege für Auslandseinsätze,* Berlin 2015.

Fouzieh Melanie Alamir, *Vernetzte Sicherheit – Quo Vadis?,* Berlin 2015.

Hartwig von Schubert, *Integrative Militärethik. Ethische Urteilsbildung in der militärischen Führung,* Berlin 2015.

Uwe Hartmann, *Hybrider Krieg als neue Bedrohung von Freiheit und Frieden. Zur Relevanz der Inneren Führung in Politik, Gesellschaft und Streitkräften,* Berlin 2015.

Klaus Beckmann, *Treue.Bürgermut.Ungehorsam. Anstöße zur Führungskultur und zum beruflichen Selbstverständnis in der Bundeswehr,* Berlin 2015.

Florian Beerenkämper, Marcel Bohnert, Anja Buresch, Sandra Matuszewski, *Der innerafghanische Friedens- und Aussöhnungsprozess,* Berlin 2016.

Martin Sebaldt, *Nicht abwehrbereit. Die Kardinalprobleme der deutschen Streitkräfte, der Offenbarungseid des Weißbuchs und die Wege aus der Gefahr,* Berlin 2017.

Militärgeschichte

Peter Heinze, *Bundeswehr „erobert" Deutschlands Osten,* Berlin 2010.

Dieter E. Kilian, *Adenauers vergessener Retter – Major Fritz Schliebusch,* Berlin 2011.

Ingo Pfeiffer, *Gegner wider Willen. Konfrontation von Volksmarine und Bundesmarine auf See,* Berlin 2012.

Ingo Pfeiffer, *Seestreitkräfte der DDR. Abriss 1950 bis 1990,* Berlin 2014

Dieter E. Kilian, *Kai-Uwe von Hassel und seine Familie. Zwischen Ostsee und Ostafrika. Militär-biographisches Mosaik,* Berlin 2013.

Peter Heinze, *Berliner Militärgeschichten,* Berlin 2013.

Ingo Pfeiffer, *Seestreitkräfte der DDR. Abriss 1950–1990,* Berlin 2014.

Ulrich C. Kleyser, *Lazare Carnot. "Le Grand Carnot". Ein Charakterbild,* Berlin 2016.

Eberhard Kliem, Kathrin Orth, *"Wir wurden wie blödsinnig vom Feind beschossen". Menschen und Schiffe in der Skagerrakschlacht 1916,* Berlin 2016.

Eberhard Birk, *"Auf Euch ruht das Heil meines theuern Württemberg!". Das Gefecht bei Tauberbischofsheim am 24. Juli 1866 im Spiegel der württembergischen Heeresgeschichte des 19. Jahrhunderts,* Berlin 2016.

Eckhard Lisec, *Der Unabhängigkeitskrieg und die Gründung der Türkei 1919–1923,* Berlin 2016.

Hans Frank, Norbert Rath, *Kommodore Rudolf Petersen. Führer der Schnellboote 1942–1945. Ein Leben in Licht und Schatten unteilbarer Verantwortung,* Berlin 2016.

Monterey Studies

Uwe Hartmann, *Carl von Clausewitz and the Making of Modern Strategy*, Potsdam 2002.

Zeljko Cepanec, *Croatia and NATO. The Stony Road to Membership*, Potsdam 2002.

Ekkehard Stemmer, *Demography and European Armed Forces*, Berlin 2006.

Sven Lange, *Revolt against the West. A Comparison of the Current War on Terror with the Boxer Rebellion in 1900-01*, Berlin 2007.

Klaus M. Brust, *Culture and the Transformation of the Bundeswehr*, Berlin 2007.

Donald Abenheim, *Soldier and Politics Transformed*, Berlin 2007.

Michael Stolzke, *The Conflict Aftermath. A Chance for Democracy: Norm Diffusion in Post-Conflict Peace Building*, Berlin 2007.

Frank Reimers, *Security Culture in Times of War. How did the Balkan War affect the Security Cultures in Germany and the United States?*, Berlin 2007.

Michael G. Lux, *Innere Führung – A Superior Concept of Leadership?*, Berlin 2009.

Marc A. Walther, *HAMAS between Violence and Pragmatism*, Berlin 2010.

Frank Hagemann, *Strategy Making in the European Union*, Berlin 2010.

Ralf Hammerstein, *Deliberalization in Jordan: the Roles of Islamists and U.S.-EU Assistance in stalled Democratization*, Berlin 2011.

Jochen Wittmann, *Auftragstaktik*, Berlin 2012.

Michael Hanisch, *On German Foreign und Security Policy. Determinants of German Military Engagement in Africa since 2011*, Berlin 2015.

Grégoire Monnet, *The Evolution of Strategic Thought Since September 11, 2001*, Berlin 2016.

http://www.miles-verlag.jimdo.com